Test Automation with Nightwatch.js

Simplify web testing with JavaScript and Node.js

Pallavi Sharma

bpb

www.bpbonline.com

First Edition 2025

Copyright © BPB Publications, India

ISBN: 978-93-65893-571

To View Complete
BPB Publications Catalogue
Scan the QR Code:

Dedicated to

***Zuzu**, my first son, our Lab (2011-2024), you are missed every day, our baby. We all miss you dearly!*

To the community of the WebDriver ecosystem, whose collaborative spirit drives innovation, and to the brilliant yet often unsung creators of open source projects who generously share their expertise with the world, empowering developers everywhere to build better software.

About the Author

Pallavi Sharma is a versatile professional with a rich experience spanning two decades. She has contributed in various capacities as an individual contributor, technical product manager, scrum master, intellectual property rights coordinator, and coach on various open source tools for test automation, programming for non-programmers throughout her career, and continues.

She is the founder at 5 Elements Learning, an e-learning organization, and Mosaic Words, a Green Literature Publishing company. She is a published author of 4 books on Selenium. She is a committer to the Selenium Project, currently with Selenium Documentation. She is an active participant in various international conferences on testing, automation, AI, and other similar areas, where she serves as a reviewer, judge, organizer, speaker, and enthusiastic attendee. She also holds various certifications in her field, interests, and passions.

Beyond her professional pursuits, Pallavi spends active time in writing, reading, traveling, nature watching, and conservation. She is dedicated to giving back to society and the environment through both her time and resources. She believes in being kind, starting with self.

About the Reviewers

❖ **Rajkumar Modake** is a senior vice president at a leading financial firm in New York, with over two decades of experience in the IT industry. His expertise spans multiple domains, including financial markets, healthcare, retail, and insurance. Starting his career as a developer, he transitioned into automation. He has excelled as an automation architect, designing robust automation frameworks from scratch using tools like Selenium, Appium, Nightwatch.js, Cypress, Playwright, Puppeteer, and WebDriverIO.

Rajkumar is passionate about advancing test automation technologies and has played a key role in driving automation excellence across large-scale enterprise environments. Alongside his core focus on automation, he has recently expanded his expertise into AI/ML initiatives, particularly in the area of generative AI.

He has been recognized with an honorary doctorate for his contributions to information technology and social services. A committed contributor to the technology community, Rajkumar actively engages in open-source projects, shares his knowledge on LinkedIn, and enjoys reviewing technical books to help others grow in their careers.

Outside of his professional endeavors, Rajkumar volunteers on weekends to teach and mentor aspiring technologists. He also values spending quality time with his wife, son, and daughter, and enjoys playing cricket, blending his love for technology with a fulfilling family life.

❖ **Jishnu Nambiar** is a senior automation engineer at Tekion with a passion for testing and finding bugs. He has worked extensively with Selenium, Nightwatch, and Appium to build effective automation solutions. He enjoys writing blogs about testing and is deeply passionate about the quality and craft of software testing.

Acknowledgement

This journey would not have been possible without the unwavering support of my family, who patiently endure me. Thank you for letting me be.

I extend my heartfelt gratitude to my editor and the technical reviewers whose keen eye for detail and commitment to excellence transformed my technical knowledge into accessible wisdom.

To the entire team at BPB Publications, thank you for believing in this project and providing the platform.

Finally, I am grateful to the open-source community whose collective brilliance makes tools of the WebDriver ecosystem possible, and to the readers whose desire to grow as automation professionals inspired every page of this handbook.

Preface

In today's fast-paced web development landscape, quality assurance has become as crucial as innovation itself. As applications grow increasingly complex with asynchronous operations and dynamic interfaces, manual testing simply cannot keep pace. This reality inspired my in-depth exploration of test automation, ultimately leading to the creation of this handbook.

Nightwatch.js captured my attention with its perfect balance of power and accessibility, leveraging Selenium WebDriver's capabilities while offering an intuitive JavaScript interface that developers naturally understand. However, I discovered a concerning gap between basic tutorials and real-world implementation, with no comprehensive resource guiding beginners through a complete learning journey.

This handbook fills that void by providing the progressive, practical guide I wish I had when starting out. Rather than a mere technical manual, it is a structured educational experience that transforms testing novices into automation professionals through hands-on learning. We begin with fundamentals and methodically build toward advanced concepts, using realistic scenarios that mirror professional environments.

What distinguishes this guide is its unwavering commitment to practicality. Every concept comes with executable code examples, troubleshooting guidance, and professional best practices. I have addressed the common pitfalls that newcomers encounter, providing solutions that prevent hours of frustration.

Whether you are a developer integrating testing into your workflow, a QA professional embracing automation, or a team lead evaluating frameworks, this handbook offers a clear path forward. My goal extends beyond teaching Nightwatch.js mechanics to instilling a quality-focused mindset that elevates everything you build.

As you progress, remember that mastery requires active practice. Experiment with the code examples, intentionally break things, and learn through doing. By the final chapter, you will possess both the technical skills and confidence to implement sophisticated test automation in any professional environment.

May the force of open source be with you!

Chapter 1: Introduction to Nightwatch- In this chapter, we explore Nightwatch.js as a powerful JavaScript-based test automation framework for web applications We examine why JavaScript is ideal for web testing, what distinguishes Nightwatch.js from other testing frameworks, and trace its development history. The topic covers Nightwatch's underlying architecture, explaining how it leverages the Selenium WebDriver API to control browsers and execute tests. A practical setup guide helps establish Nightwatch in your development environment.

Chapter 2: Understand the Web Applications used in the Book- In this chapter, we introduce the specific web applications that serve as examples throughout the book, detailing their features and the particular testing scenarios we will tackle with each one. These real-world applications provide the context needed to understand how Nightwatch effectively automates testing for various web components and user interactions.

Chapter 3: Getting Started with Nightwatch- This chapter guides you through setting up and configuring Nightwatch.js within Visual Studio Code for effective test automation. We explore the folder structure and essential files created during Nightwatch installation, providing insights into their purposes and interactions.

Chapter 4: Setting Visual Studio Code with Nightwatch- This chapter demonstrates how to configure your test environment in VS Code, including setting up proper project structures and installing necessary extensions for enhanced JavaScript testing capabilities. You will learn how to establish and manage test global variables that can be accessed throughout your test suite, streamlining test development and maintenance.

Chapter 5: Identifying Elements- This chapter explores the fundamental concepts essential for effective Nightwatch.js test automation. We begin by examining selectors, the mechanisms used to identify and target specific elements within web pages, and the various selector types supported by Nightwatch, including CSS, XPath, and ID selectors. Through practical examples, you will learn how to create precise selectors for different web elements across various scenarios.

Chapter 6: Interacting with Web Elements- This chapter explains why interaction with web elements is crucial for mimicking user behavior and verifying application functionality. We cover the diverse interaction types available in Nightwatch, from clicks and text input to drag-and-drop operations and keyboard events. The topic details specific commands for implementing these interactions effectively in your test scripts.

Chapter 7: Synchronization- In this chapter, we address the critical concept of synchronization, how Nightwatch manages timing between test steps to ensure reliable execution despite varying page load times and dynamic content. Understanding these core concepts provides the foundation needed to create robust, reliable automated tests with Nightwatch.js.

Chapter 8: Assertions in Nightwatch- This chapter explores verification essentials in Nightwatch.js automated testing. We examine Nightwatch's Command Queue architecture that manages sequential command execution and timing dependencies through callback functions. You will learn about wait commands that ensure elements are ready for interaction and discover the variety of assertion commands available for validating element properties and states. The section covers Nightwatch's 'expect' interface, which provides chainable syntax for intuitive verification of actions and conditions.

Chapter 9: Working with Form Elements- In this chapter, you will learn how to automate form elements using Nightwatch. You will learn about HTML elements and form components like text fields, drop-downs, checkboxes, and radio buttons. The chapter includes hands-on examples and ends with a complete user registration script that demonstrates practical form automation techniques with proper validations.

Chapter 10: Working with Tables, Drop-downs, Frames and Alerts- In this chapter, we learn four essential web elements: tables, drop-downs, iFrames, and JavaScript alerts. You will learn to dynamically traverse HTML tables to extract product data, handle dropdown lists by fetching and validating options, work with embedded iFrames by switching contexts, and manage all three types of JavaScript popups (Alert, Confirm, and Prompt). Each section includes practical examples with complete working scripts using real test applications, giving you the tools to handle these common web elements in any automation scenario.

Chapter 11: Browser Logs, Page Performance, Capture Screenshots, and Actions- This chapter covers advanced Nightwatch techniques, including capturing browser logs for debugging, measuring page performance metrics, taking automated screenshots, and handling complex user actions like right-click, hover, and drag-and-drop. You will learn practical configuration steps and gain tools for sophisticated automation scenarios with complete working examples.

Chapter 12: Page Objects- In this chapter the Page Object Model design pattern is introduced, that separates test logic from application elements, making your automation code more maintainable. You will learn to create reusable page objects through a complete login/logout example, organizing selectors and actions into structured files that reduce code duplication and simplify maintenance when applications change.

Chapter 13: Managing Data Using Excel and CSV Files- In this chapter, you learn to separate test data from your automation scripts by using external data files. You will learn to read and write both CSV and Excel files using Node.js modules, create reusable data reader functions, and build data-driven tests that iterate through multiple sets of credentials. The chapter includes complete examples of login/logout scenarios that automatically run for each row of data, demonstrating how to make your tests more flexible and maintainable by managing test data externally.

Chapter 14: Learn About Logs, and Screenshots Management- In this chapter, you will learn to build debugging capabilities through logging and screenshot management. You will learn to use the Winston library for structured logging, capture screenshots at key points and failures, and integrate these tools with your existing tests. The chapter shows how to transform unclear test failures into actionable debugging information with comprehensive logs and visual evidence.

Chapter 15: Execution of Tests in BrowserStack- This chapter will guide you through integrating Nightwatch.js with BrowserStack's cloud-based testing platform to execute automated tests across multiple browsers, operating systems, and devices without maintaining local infrastructure. You will learn to set up your BrowserStack account, configure Nightwatch for cloud execution, and run tests simultaneously on different environments like Windows Chrome, Mac Safari, and mobile browsers. The chapter includes practical examples and step-by-step instructions for viewing detailed test results through BrowserStack's dashboard, enabling you to ensure consistent application performance across all user platforms.

Code Bundle and Coloured Images

Please follow the link to download the
Code Bundle and the *Coloured Images* of the book:

https://rebrand.ly/d7b663

The code bundle for the book is also hosted on GitHub at
https://github.com/bpbpublications/Test-Automation-with-Nightwatch.js.
In case there's an update to the code, it will be updated on the existing GitHub repository.

We have code bundles from our rich catalogue of books and videos available at
https://github.com/bpbpublications. Check them out!

Errata

We take immense pride in our work at BPB Publications and follow best practices to ensure the accuracy of our content to provide with an indulging reading experience to our subscribers. Our readers are our mirrors, and we use their inputs to reflect and improve upon human errors, if any, that may have occurred during the publishing processes involved. To let us maintain the quality and help us reach out to any readers who might be having difficulties due to any unforeseen errors, please write to us at :

errata@bpbonline.com

Your support, suggestions and feedbacks are highly appreciated by the BPB Publications' Family.

Did you know that BPB offers eBook versions of every book published, with PDF and ePub files available? You can upgrade to the eBook version at www.bpbonline. com and as a print book customer, you are entitled to a discount on the eBook copy. Get in touch with us at :

business@bpbonline.com for more details.

At **www.bpbonline.com**, you can also read a collection of free technical articles, sign up for a range of free newsletters, and receive exclusive discounts and offers on BPB books and eBooks.

Piracy

If you come across any illegal copies of our works in any form on the internet, we would be grateful if you would provide us with the location address or website name. Please contact us at **business@bpbonline.com** with a link to the material.

If you are interested in becoming an author

If there is a topic that you have expertise in, and you are interested in either writing or contributing to a book, please visit **www.bpbonline.com**. We have worked with thousands of developers and tech professionals, just like you, to help them share their insights with the global tech community. You can make a general application, apply for a specific hot topic that we are recruiting an author for, or submit your own idea.

Reviews

Please leave a review. Once you have read and used this book, why not leave a review on the site that you purchased it from? Potential readers can then see and use your unbiased opinion to make purchase decisions. We at BPB can understand what you think about our products, and our authors can see your feedback on their book. Thank you!

For more information about BPB, please visit **www.bpbonline.com**.

Join our book's Discord space

Join the book's Discord Workspace for Latest updates, Offers, Tech happenings around the world, New Release and Sessions with the Authors:

https://discord.bpbonline.com

Table of Contents

CHAPTER 1
Introduction to Nightwatch

The world of the web is getting complex as you read this statement. The users of the web have too much content to consume in a short span of time and lack the patience to wait for your application to provide what they want, and where they want the data. We have available at our disposal all kinds of applications, from health trackers to travel booking, everything is now at the click of our fingers. There are more creators of every kind of application, and each is competitive for their segments' user base attention. The demand for the application to be available on the desktop and on the watch is not even a question; it is a norm now. A world where notifications are the way to tell the time of day, and if you do not receive that good morning message in the group, you start getting panic attacks. Yes, welcome to the world of hyper connectivity. In more than one way, we have JavaScript to thank for it.

As the release cycles of the software get shorter, there is a significant shift in testing of the applications being created as well. Cumbersome libraries which require significant setup do not serve the purpose where the developers are looking for solutions which can work with the tools and environments they are already using. This has led to a surge in various test automation tools, libraries, and frameworks available now which are JavaScript based. This book assumes you are already familiar with JavaScript, and with that context set, we will dive into the details and usage of Nightwatch as the test automation framework for web applications and websites.

Structure

In this chapter, we will discuss the following topics:

- JavaScript for test automation for web applications
- Understanding Nightwatch
- History of Nightwatch
- Working of Nightwatch
- Setting up Nightwatch

Objectives

After completing this chapter, you will be able to understand why to use JavaScript test automation framework for web applications. You will also understand what is Nightwatch, its history, and how it works. By the end of this chapter, you will also learn how to set up Nightwatch in your system.

JavaScript for test automation for web applications

JavaScript is the most in-demand programming language for web development in world, as per survey by stackoverflow (**https://survey.stackoverflow.co/2024/technology/#1-programming-scripting-and-markup-languages**). Since the advent of dynamic, interactive web applications, JavaScript popularity has soared. And with that, various front-end frameworks for web development are now available like Angular, ReactJS, and Vue.js. You can find their names and popularity from the latest survey by State of JS here: **https://2023.stateofjs.com/en-US/libraries/front-end-frameworks/**. As the application undergoes the development process, testing gets integrated into it at various levels from unit test to integrated, to system, and finally the end-to-end testing of the web application.

There are many JavaScript-based testing tools and frameworks available in the market for end-to-end web automation, and they have gained significant popularity and acceptance by the community of JavaScript developers and users. The following table lists them:

S.no	Name	Details	Link
1	Selenium	The most popular web automation tool. It is an umbrella project which has Selenium IDE, Selenium WebDriver, and Selenium Grid. It supports multiple programming languages, JavaScript is one of them.	**https://www.selenium.dev/**

S.no	Name	Details	Link
2	Jest	It is a JavaScript based testing framework that supports various JavaScript libraries like Angular, Vue, React. It is the most popular JavaScript testing framework.	**https://jestjs.io/**
3	Puppeteer	It is a JavaScript library which allows you to automate chrome/chromium-based browser and firefox browser.	**https://pptr.dev/**
4	Nightwatch	It is a framework to automate the testing of web applications and native mobile applications. One of the most popular JavaScript based test automation framework.	**https://nightwatchjs. org/**
5	Playwright	It is a framework for end-to-end testing of web applications.	**https://playwright.dev/**
6	Jasmine	It is a behavior driven development framework for testing the JavaScript code written.	**https://jasmine.github. io/**
7	Cypress	It is a JavaScript based end-to-end web testing tool which is primarily focused to be used by the developers.	**https://www.cypress. io/**

Table 1.1: JavaScript based test automation libraries and frameworks

People who use JavaScript and JavaScript-based technologies for web development use one of the above-listed tools or frameworks to test their applications. Let us now have a look at Nightwatch, one of the most popular JavaScript-based test automation frameworks.

Understanding Nightwatch

Nightwatch is a test automation framework to test web applications and web sites. It is written in Node.js and allows us to perform end to end testing of the application across all major browsers, through the usage of the W3C WebDriver API. It is an open-source tool, whose development is now supported by the Browser Stack organization through its open-source program office, headed by *David Burns*. The current version of Nightwatch available is the version 3.x series, at the time of writing this book. The thought behind Nightwatch is to provide an out-of-the-box solution for testing web applications, which do not require other libraries, dependencies, or configurations to be set up. The end user can focus on writing tests, of different types as follows:

- End-to-end test for web applications, which will run for all major browsers
- Unit test for Node.js service
- Integration test for HTTP APIs

The official website of Nightwatch is: **https://nightwatchjs.org/**

History of Nightwatch

Nightwatch was initially created by *Andrei Rusu*, in 2014, from Pineview Labs. The tool was created with the mindset of a ready-to-go solution that requires less setup through additional libraries and configuration requirements. In the year 2021, it was acquired by Browserstack: **https://www.linkedin.com/pulse/browserstack-acquires-nightwatchjs-leading-test-automation-arora/**. Being open-source, Nightwatch is driven by community, and more details about the project and if you wish to be part of its growing community can be found here: **https://nightwatchjs.org/about/community/**

Working of Nightwatch

Nightwatch is a **command-line interface** (**CLI**) tool built over the W3C WebDriver API. The WebDriver is part of the Selenium (**http://www.selenium.dev**) project. It is a library for automating web browsers. It is recognized as a W3C specification. The WebDriver provides a protocol to remotely control the web browser through restful HTTP API. More details about it are available here: **https://www.w3.org/TR/webdriver1/**. Any major browser that is W3C compliant will allow browser automation using the WebDriver. Thus, Nightwatch supports automation of all major browsers.

The following figure shows the flow of commands from Nightwatch through WebDriver to the browser for test purposes:

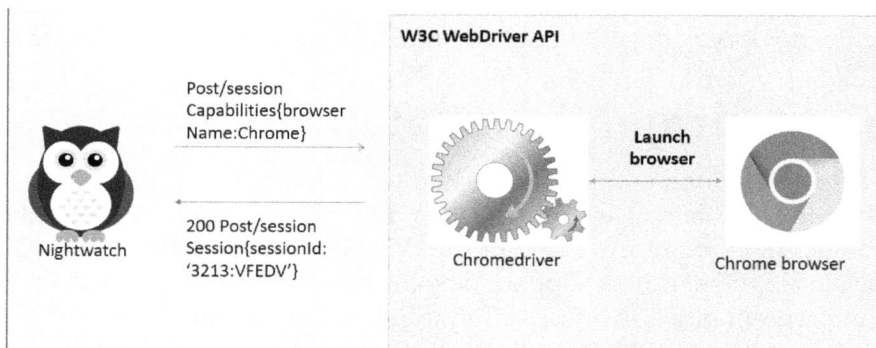

Figure 1.1: How Nightwatch works

As per the preceding figure, Nightwatch uses the WebDriver API to manage the browsers. It automates all the major browsers—Chrome, Edge, Safari, and Firefox.

Here, we also need to understand that while WebDriver API, a component of Selenium, is a library, it automates the browser, Nightwatch is an integrated framework written in Node.js. It was created to test web applications. Let us now look at how to set up Nightwatch on the system.

Setting up Nightwatch

To set up Nightwatch in the system, we need to first ensure we have Node.js installed on the system. We can install Node.js from: **https://nodejs.org/en**. Create a new project on your system and open the command line interface from there. For this book, our project structure is as:

```
D:\WORK\BPB PUBLICATIONS\NIGHTWATCH\TestProjectNW
```

Note: The path used is as per the author's system. Your path may change depending on your work system.

After we have ensured we have Node.js we need to follow these steps to set up Nightwatch in our system:

1. Open the command line interface and go to the above-mentioned location, please note the location could be different as per your system and as you have created.

2. Once in that location, run the command - `:/> npm init nightwatch`

3. When we run the above-mentioned command, we will see the configuration wizard getting started as follows:

    Note: The version of Nightwatch used in this book is v3. Be aware that in the open-source world, a software version changes, which can result in some steps or concepts being changed. Always refer to the main website of Nightwatch for any clarifications and information on the latest version.

```
D:\WORK\BPB PUBLICATIONS\NIGHTWATCH\TestProjectNW>npm init nightwatch

  | \ | |(_)      | |   | |                    | |        | |
  | \| | _  __ _  | |__ | |_ _      __ __ _  _ | |_  ___  | |__
  | . ` || |/ _` || '_ \ | __\ \ /\ / // _` || __|/ __| | '_ \
  | |\ || || (_| || | | || |_ \ V  V /| (_| || |_| (__  | | | |
  \_| \_/|_| \__, ||_| |_| \__| \_/\_/  \__,_| \__|\___| |_| |_|
              __/ |
             |___/

package.json not found in the root directory. Initializing a new NPM project..

Wrote to D:\WORK\BPB PUBLICATIONS\NIGHTWATCH\TestProjectNW\package.json:

{
  "name": "testprojectnw",
  "version": "1.0.0",
  "description": "",
  "main": "index.js",
  "scripts": {
    "test": "echo \"Error: no test specified\" && exit 1"
  },
  "keywords": [],
  "author": "",
  "license": "ISC"
}


================================
Nightwatch Configuration Wizard
================================
```

Figure 1.2: Nightwatch configuration wizard

4. The first question it will ask is what type of project we want to set; we will choose **End-to-End testing** as shown in the following figure:

```
Setting up Nightwatch in D:\WORK\BPB PUBLICATIONS\NIGHTWATCH\TestProjectNW...

? Select testing type to setup for your project (Press <space> to select, <a> to toggle all, <i> to invert selection, and <enter> to proceed)
>(*) End-to-End testing
 ( ) Component testing
 ( ) Mobile app testing
```

Figure 1.3: Selecting project type

5. It will then select the test runner for the project, for which we will choose **JavaScript**:

```
? Select language + test runner variant (Use arrow keys)
> JavaScript / default
  TypeScript / default
  JavaScript / Mocha
  JavaScript / CucumberJS
```

Figure 1.4: Selecting language and test runner for project

6. The next step will be to select the browsers on which we want our tests to run. Here, we select all the browsers:

```
? Select target browsers (Press  space  to select,  <a>  to toggle all, <i> to invert selection, and  enter  to proceed)
>(*) Chrome
 ( ) Firefox
 ( ) Edge
```

Figure 1.5: Selecting browsers for test execution

7. It will then prompt us to enter the name of the folder where the test will be stored, by default it will be test. We are not changing that.

```
? Enter source folder where test files are stored (test)
```

Figure 1.6: Selecting folder for test files

8. The next step is to provide the base URL of the project, for us it will be: **http://practice.bpbonline.com/**.

```
? Enter the base_url of the project http://practice.bpbonline.com/
```

Figure 1.7: Provide base URL of the project

9. The next step is determining where we want the Nightwatch test execution to occur: locally or remotely. We will select **Both**:

```
? Select where to run Nightwatch tests
  On localhost
  On a remote/cloud service
> Both
```

Figure 1.8: Execution of tests

10. Next, select the cloud provider. You can choose either. In this chapter, we are selecting BrowserStack, as its company is now behind the NightWatch project.

```
? (Remote) Select cloud provider:
  BrowserStack
  Sauce Labs
> Other providers or remote selenium-server
```

Figure 1.9: Selecting a cloud provider

Note: If you select to run on your own remote selenium server or any other cloud provider, you will have to manually configure the host and port details in the nightwatch.conf.js file.

11. Next, we will collect usage metrics, which can be set to no, and for mobile applications, which is also set to no. After this, the Nightwatch installation will start as shown in the following figure:

```
? Allow Nightwatch to collect completely anonymous usage metrics? (y/N) N
```

Figure 1.10: Choosing collection of anonymous metrics

12. Finally, it will ask you if you wish to setup for mobile devices as well, for the context of the book we will select it as no.

```
? Setup testing on Mobile devices as well? (Use arrow keys)
  Yes
> No, skip for now
```

Figure 1.11: Setup for mobile devices

13. Once the setup is complete you will receive a success message, mentioning about the version of the Nightwatch installed.

```
✦ SETUP COMPLETE

  Nightwatch:
    version: 3.2.1
    changelog: https://github.com/nightwatchjs/nightwatch/releases/tag/v3.2.1

  Join our Discord community to find answers to your issues or queries. Or just join and say hi.
  https://discord.gg/SN8Da2X

✗ RUN EXAMPLE TESTS

To run all examples, run:
  npx nightwatch .\nightwatch\examples

To run a single example (ecosia.js), run:
  npx nightwatch .\nightwatch\examples\basic\ecosia.js

Note: Microsoft Edge Webdriver is not installed automatically.
Please follow the below link ("Download" and "Standalone Usage" sections) to setup EdgeDriver manually:
  https://nightwatchjs.org/guide/browser-drivers-setup/edgedriver.html
```

Figure 1.12: Setup of Nightwatch complete

You will also notice some new folders being created in the project folder structure as follows:

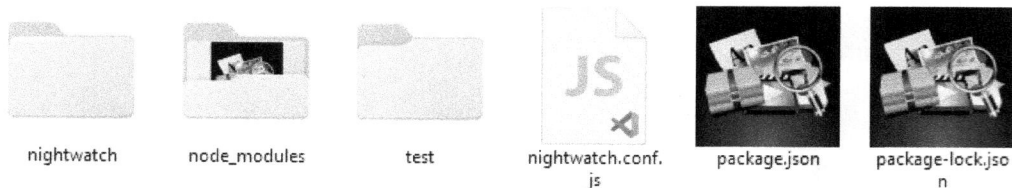

| nightwatch | node_modules | test | nightwatch.conf.js | package.json | package-lock.json |

Figure 1.13: Project structure after Nightwatch setup

The explanation of the folder structure created will be discussed in the upcoming chapter.

To verify if everything works fine, we can run a simple test example that is provided by default by the Nightwatch setup. It is available in the **nightwatch\examples\basic** folder. The name of the file is ecosia.js. The test script content looks as follows:

```
1. describe('Ecosia.org Demo', function() {
2.   before(browser => browser.navigateTo('https://www.ecosia.org/'));
```

```
3.   it('Demo test ecosia.org', function(browser) {
4.     browser
5.       .waitForElementVisible('body')
6.       .assert.titleContains('Ecosia')
7.       .assert.visible('input[type=search]')
8.       .setValue('input[type=search]', 'nightwatch')
9.       .assert.visible('button[type=submit]')
10.      .click('button[type=submit]')
11.      .assert.textContains('.layout__content', 'Nightwatch.js');
12.  });
13.  after(browser => browser.end());
14.});
```

We execute the preceding code by typing the following command in the command line interface-

npx nightwatch .\nightwatch\examples\basic\ecosia.js

As we execute the command, we will find the Chrome browser launched with the URL: **http://www.ecosia.org**. It will then perform the search for text **nightwatch**, and perform an assertion whether the content displayed after search contains Nightwatch.js or not. If the text exists, the test will pass; otherwise, it will fail. Finally, the browser will quit. We will see the following image as test execution starts:

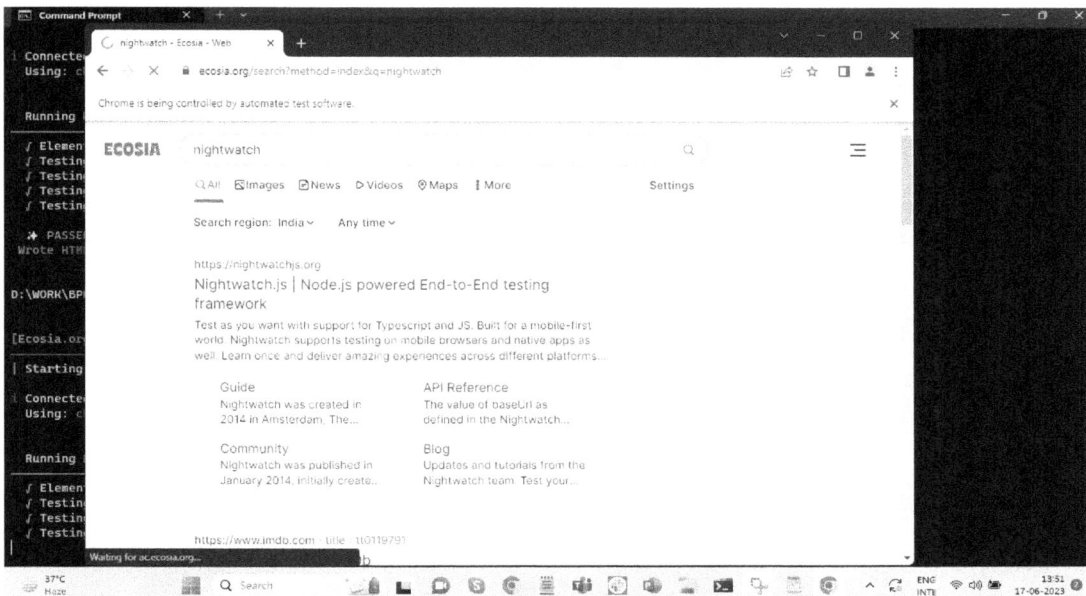

Figure 1.14: Ecosia web application example test

Thus, we can conclude that Nightwatch was successfully installed. If you are a Selenium user, you can appreciate the ease with which you were able to quickly set up Nightwatch. The configuration wizard made things easy, and the sample example folders give a good starting point for new users.

Conclusion

In this chapter, we have explored why JavaScript-based applications have gained popularity. We discussed the various JavaScript-based development frameworks available. We understood the need for test frameworks for web applications that require less management and configuration handling. We understood what Nightwatch is, the history of Nightwatch and how to setup Nightwatch on system. We also saw the other JavaScript based testing frameworks and libraries available out in the market.

In the next chapter, we will have a look at the different types of web application, which will be used across the chapters of the book to understand concepts. The scenarios from these web applications will also be used to create test scripts to understand and implement Nightwatch concepts.

Questions

1. What is Nightwatch?
2. What is WebDriver API?
3. Who created Nightwatch?

Answers

1. Nightwatch is an integrated test automation framework for complete end to end testing of web applications.

2. WebDriver API is a component of Selenium and a W3C specification. It is a library which supports automation of web browsers by remotely controlling them protocol based on restful HTTP API.

3. Nightwatch was created by *Andrei Rusu*.

Join our book's Discord space

Join the book's Discord Workspace for Latest updates, Offers, Tech happenings around the world, New Release and Sessions with the Authors:

https://discord.bpbonline.com

CHAPTER 2

Understanding the Web Applications used in the Book

It is surprising to note that only three decades ago the world wide web was born when *Tim Berner-Lee* at CERN published the first website. In such a short period of time we have crossed 1.8 billion websites. The world of web is ever changing, with new technologies, new languages, and new tools now available at our disposal. These tools help in the creation of websites, which become the interface of our business to end users. The end user experience should be error free, for this testing is crucial. Different websites have different usages of technology and as testers, when we are learning about a new tool, it is important that we try to select a few applications on which we will learn different aspects of the tool's working.

In this chapter, as we continue our journey of learning Nightwatch, we will pick a few web applications and select scenarios in them that allow us to explore and implement our learnings of the tool in the upcoming chapters.

Note: This book assumes that you have pre-existing knowledge of testing, but little or no knowledge of WebDriver (Selenium), so we will be covering the concepts around it in Chapters 5, 6, and 7 of this book.

For now, let us explore the web applications we will use throughout the book.

Structure

In this chapter, we will discuss the following topics:

- Overview of web applications

- Walkthrough of application 1: Practice BPB application
- Walkthrough of application 2: Internet Heroku application

Objectives

After completing this chapter, you will be able to understand the applications used in the book. You will also understand the scenarios in the applications, which we will explore for testing using Nightwatch.

Overview of web applications

The world of the web is complex; there are all kinds of web applications one can find. Simple web applications of one page, to a web application which span multiple pages. Some applications are static in nature, while others are dynamic. Some applications are responsive by design, and some do not have the same features. As a tester, we get to see and come across all these kinds of web applications, and then to add to the complexity is the business domain to which they belong to. As mentioned earlier in the chapter, there are around 1.8 billion web applications accounted for as per the last statistics. The following figure illustrates it:

How Many Websites Are There?
Number of websites online from 1991 to 2021

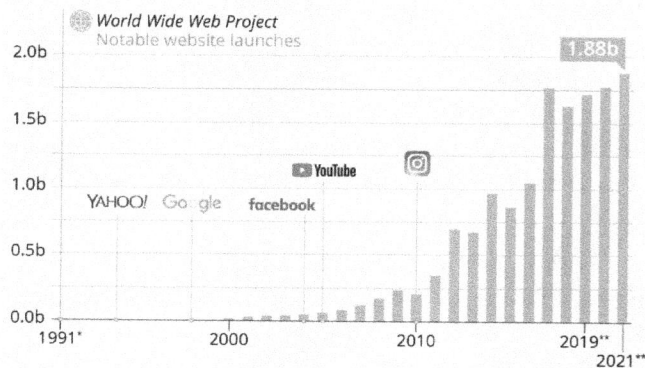

World Wide Web Project
Notable website launches

2.0b ··· 1.88b

1.5b

1.0b ▶YouTube ◎
YAHOO! Go gle facebook

0.5b

0.0b
1991*   2000   2010   2019**
                                                  2021**

*   As of August 1, 1991.
** Latest available data for 2019: October 28, for 2020: June 2, for 2021: August 6.
Source: Internet Live Stats

Figure 2.1: Web application statistics

The number of tools available in the market, besides the human mind, to automate the process of testing web applications has also seen a significant increase in trend. In this book, our tool of choice is Nightwatch, and it uses WebDriver (Selenium) under the hood to automate the browser, which we learned about in *Chapter 1, Introduction to Nightwatch.*

As we learn about the tool, it is crucial that we carefully pick the applications that provide us with enough scope to explore our test automation skills. We will pick up these skills in a structured manner so that we do not get lost in the humongous web out there. Keeping that in mind, let us explore the two applications we will be using in this book. Please note that you are free to choose or select any other as well for your learning journey.

Walkthrough of application 1: Practice BPB application

The first application that we will see in the book is an e-commerce application. The URL of the application is: **http://practice.bpbonline.com/**. This application has various scenarios to explore and provides us with ample situations for testing. New user creation, ordering multiple products, and verifying account login, to name a few. This application also provides us a platform to explore different types of web elements, and we can learn how using the WebDriver on which Nightwatch is based we can automate them. Before we get into the nitty-gritty of automating the testing of the web application, let us first learn about the web application at hand.

The following figure shows us the home screen of the application:

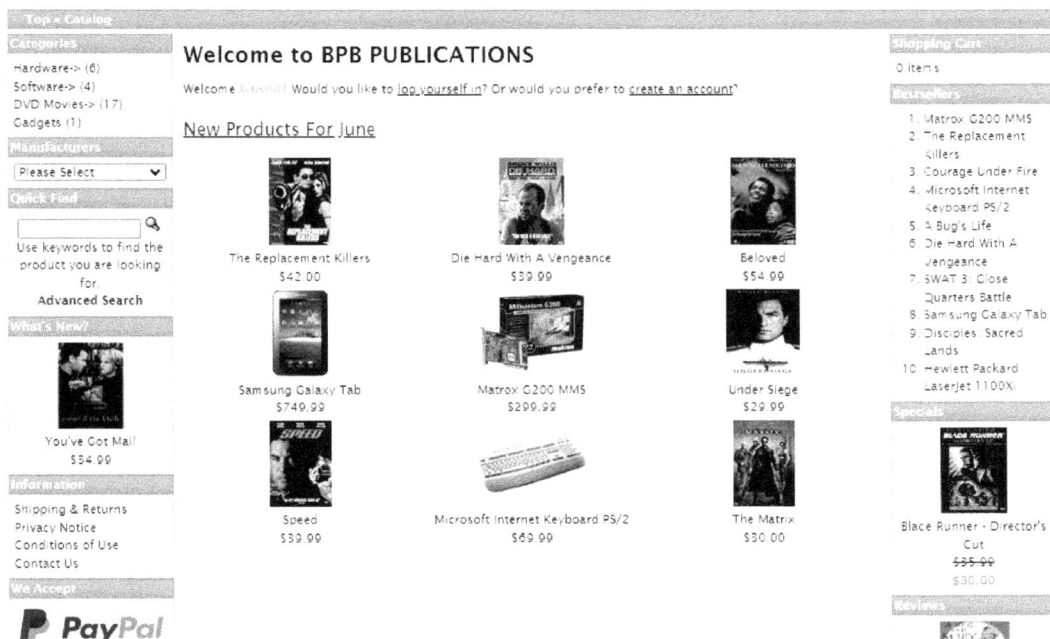

Figure 2.2: Practice BPB application

The application allows us to perform some scenarios, which we will also be picking for testing in the upcoming chapters. Listing some scenarios in the following table:

S.No.	Scenario	Explanation
1.	Register user	As a new user, we need to register to the application, so that we can have an account. We will also be able to place dummy orders once we are registered users.
2.	Login	As a registered user, we should be able to successfully login and logout of the application. If we are not registered, then we should not be able to login.
3.	Search product	As a visitor to the website, whether registered user or not, we should be able to search for the products. There are various scenarios which can be created from here. It also covers Advance Search.
4.	Order product	As a registered user, we should be able to place a dummy order for one or multiple products.
5.	Change details	As a registered user, we should be able to change our details like phone number, address from the account section.

Table 2.1: Scenarios from the BPB application practice

As we learn different concepts like data-driven testing, we will pick up Search Product from the above table, list down its steps in the upcoming chapters, and learn how to use Nightwatch to create a test case script to automate the process. A good starting point for this chapter will be to register yourself as a user to the application, and then keep the username and password handy as you explore the chapters of the book. To register yourself as a user, perform these steps:

1. Open the application, and click on **My Account** as shown in the following figure:

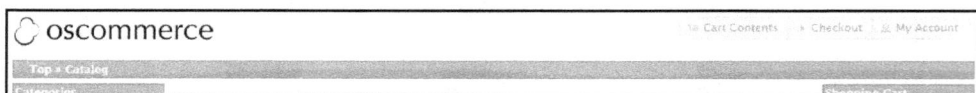

Figure 2.3: Click My Account on Home Page

2. On the Welcome/Sign in page, click on the **Continue** button, for the **New Customer** as shown in the following figure:

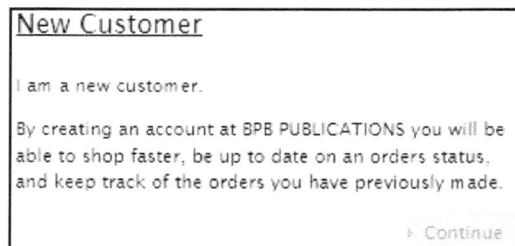

Figure 2.4: Click on Continue button for register user

3. Fill all the mandatory fields of the form which are marked with *. Remember to use a dummy email address. Save this email address and password where you will remember.

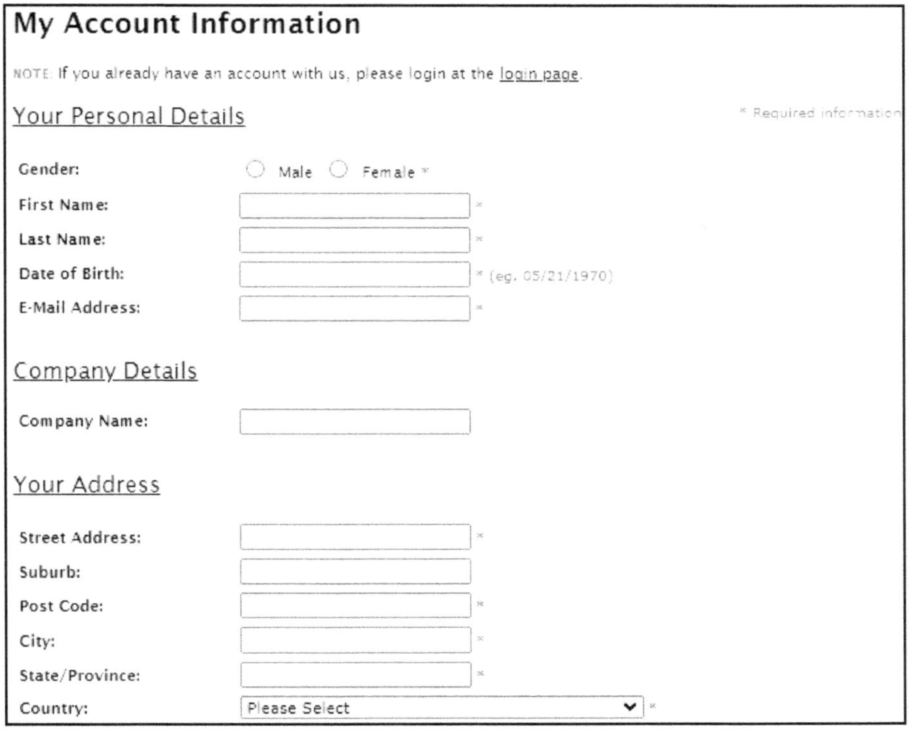

My Account Information

NOTE: If you already have an account with us, please login at the login page.

Your Personal Details

* Required information

Gender: ⭕ Male ⭕ Female *

First Name: [   ] *

Last Name: [   ] *

Date of Birth: [   ] * (eg. 05/21/1970)

E-Mail Address: [   ] *

Company Details

Company Name: [   ]

Your Address

Street Address: [   ] *

Suburb: [   ]

Post Code: [   ] *

City: [   ] *

State/Province: [   ] *

Country: [Please Select ▾] *

Figure 2.5: Account creation page

4. Once you have added information about all the important fields, and click on the continue button in the end, it will take you to the page which shows that your account is created.

Your Account Has Been Created!

Congratulations! Your new account has been successfully created! You can now take advantage of member priviledges to enhance your online shopping experience with us. If you have ANY questions about the operation of this online shop, please email the store owner.

A confirmation has been sent to the provided email address. If you have not received it within the hour, please contact us.

> Continue

Figure 2.6: Successful account creation

5. You can now explore the application as a registered user, or **Log Off** from the application by clicking on the **Log Off** link as shown in the following figure:

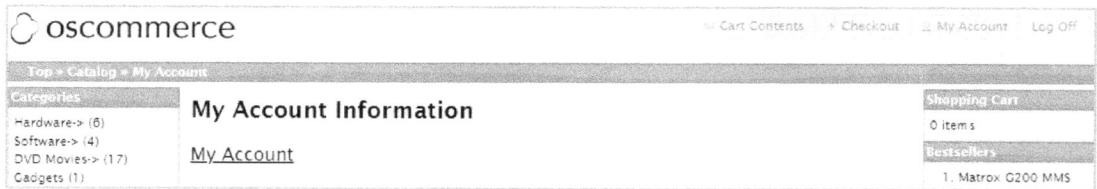

Figure 2.7: Log Off link

Thus, with the above steps, we have successfully registered as a user to the application. We will now be able to explore all the application scenarios completely for testing purposes.

Let us now have a look at the next web application.

Walkthrough of application 2: Internet Heroku application

The Internet Heroku web application URL is: **https://the-internet.herokuapp.com/**. This web application is powered by Elemental Selenium (**https://elementalselenium.com/**). Previously maintained by *Dave Haffener*, it is now supported by Sauce Labs. The benefit of this application is that it makes individual pages of various web elements available which you can use to test in silos using Nightwatch. The home page of the application looks as follows:

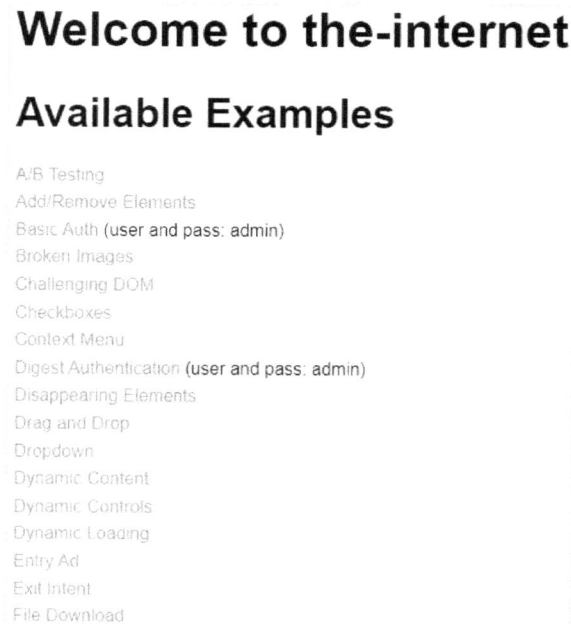

Figure 2.8: Internet Heroku web application

The benefit of this website is that it lists many scenarios for test automation like, file upload, dynamic element handling, JavaScript alerts, etc. Learning by automating the examples from this web application benefits any beginner. With Sauce Labs now backing it, you can also contribute to the website, add scenarios, or even run it locally. If that interests you, go ahead and learn more about it here: **https://github.com/saucelabs/elemental-next**.

As we come across handling different types of web elements testing and how to automate it in the book, we will pick some of the scenarios from this application. We will explain those scenarios in the chapter, as and where we pick them.

Conclusion

In this chapter, we saw the two applications we will pick to learn about Nightwatch in this book. We are also learned how to test some of their scenarios, and understood the fact that we can explore other applications as well for our learning journey.

In the next chapter, we will learn about setting up Nightwatch in the system and configuring the environment for the creation of scripts and execution.

Questions

1. Who created the first website?
2. Which company now owns the Elemental Selenium website?

Answers

1. Tim Lee-Berner at CERN created the first website
2. Sauce Labs

Join our book's Discord space

Join the book's Discord Workspace for Latest updates, Offers, Tech happenings around the world, New Release and Sessions with the Authors:

https://discord.bpbonline.com

CHAPTER 3

Getting Started with Nightwatch

In the earlier chapters, we have seen what Nightwatch is and how we set up our system. We also ran a basic test to verify the setup and learned about various web applications that will be used throughout the book to create various test scenarios. In this chapter, we will understand different building blocks of Nightwatch so that we can use it well to automate the test scenarios and speed up our testing process. We will first understand the basic folder structure that Nightwatch creates as it gets installed in the system. Further, we will cover a few generic concepts of Nightwatch which act at configuration level for designing tests. Finally, we will move on to understanding concepts that will help us write the actual test script with Nightwatch.

Structure

This chapter will discuss the following topics:

- File structure created by Nightwatch
- Configuring the test environment
- Configuring the test global variables

Objectives

After reading this chapter, you will be able to understand the folder structure and files Nightwatch creates when we install it in the system. You will also be able to configure the test environment and the test global variables.

File structure created by Nightwatch

In *Chapter 1, Introduction to Nightwatch,* we learned about Nightwatch and how to install it in the system. In this section, we will look at the folder structure and the files Nightwatch creates after installation. Your screen will look like the following figure:

Figure 3.1: Nightwatch folder and file structure after installation

Each of these folders and files created during the Nightwatch installation in the system has a special function. Through the following table, let us have a look at it:

S.No.	Name	Folder/ File	Description
1.	nightwatch	Folder	This is the main folder that gets created. It has the main sub folder examples. In this folder, we have some sample codes which help us get started with Nightwatch. The other sub folders created here, like page-objects, exist to support the code samples in the examples folder.
2.	node_ modules	Folder	This sub folder contains the different npm modules which the default Nightwatch requires.
3.	test	Folder	The test folder, initially empty, is where we store the test files we create.
4.	test_output	Folder	The test_output folder has the HTML report which gets generated on the test execution by Nightwatch.
5.	nightwatch. conf.js	File	This is the configuration file at the tool Nightwatch level. We can modify this to add, delete, or modify information with respect to the test scenarios we have for our application under test.
6.	package.json	File	It is a default .json file which contains metadata information about the project like author, version, and browser versions at the time of Nightwatch installation.
7.	package- lock.json	File	This file contains information of all the node modules, and their versions, on which Nightwatch is dependent. It helps the future devs know the dependencies. This file is automatically generated.

Table 3.1: Nightwatch folder/file information after installation in system

We will now move on to understanding how to configure the test environment for testing the web application.

Configuring the test environment

When setting up our environment for test automation, it is imperative to have the metadata file available, which holds the key details of the automation suite configuration. For example, the default URL of the web application under test, the browser versions to be used, what browsers to execute the test on, the location from where to pick test data, page object information location, and similar things. This configuration file can also hold within itself the global variables information which helps capture the common variable details that all tests in the test automation suite can use. When we install Nightwatch in the system, by default, the nightwatch.conf.js file gets created. Let us explore this file to understand its content. We need to note down in here that this file will create the default content which Nightwatch generated based on the installation settings we performed while setting it on the system. We should also note that we can modify the settings in this file as per our requirements for test execution which can change over time. Let us explore the configuration file, section by section:

module_export

In the first section, the file displays information about the modules, which contains information details of the path of folders and sub folders created at the time of installing Nightwatch:

```
module export=
(property) export=: {
src_folders: string[];
page_objects_path: string[];
custom_commands_path: string[];
custom_assertions_path: string[];
plugins: never[];
globals_path: string;
webdriver: {};
test_workers: {
enabled: boolean;
};
test_settings: {
...;
};
}
```

If we look at the configuration file, the actual content that will be present is as follows:

```
module.exports = {
  // An array of folders (excluding subfolders) where your tests are
located;
  // if this is not specified, the test source must be passed as the second
argument to the test runner.
  src_folders: ['test','nightwatch/examples'],

  // See https://nightwatchjs.org/guide/concepts/page-object-model.html
  page_objects_path: ['nightwatch/page-objects'],

  // See https://nightwatchjs.org/guide/extending-nightwatch/adding-custom-
commands.html
  custom_commands_path: ['nightwatch/custom-commands'],

  // See https://nightwatchjs.org/guide/extending-nightwatch/adding-custom-
assertions.html
  custom_assertions_path: ['nightwatch/custom-assertions'],

  // See https://nightwatchjs.org/guide/extending-nightwatch/adding-
plugins.html
  plugins: [],

  // See https://nightwatchjs.org/guide/concepts/test-globals.html
  globals_path: '',

  webdriver: {},

  test_workers: {
    enabled: true
  },
```

The path of these modules is from the **nightwatch** folder of our project. The following figure displays that:

custom-assertion   custom-comma   examples   page-objects   templates
s   nds

Figure 3.2: Subfolders of the nightwatch main folder

As shown in the preceding code, we see a heading of **globals_path**. This key data can hold the value of the path of the file that contains information about the global variables. For example, **"globals_path": "lib/globals.js"**. We can change the name of this to **globals** and create the global variable here itself. The following shows an example:

```
"globals": {
    "username" : "admin",
    "password" : "admin"
```

As we can see above, we have created two key value pairs that have two global variables username and password with their values set in there. In our test scripts wherever we use these global variables, the values **"admin"** will be used. Our test scripts can and will have local variables as well. Let us now have a look at the next section of the configuration file:

```
test_settings: {
default: {
disable_error_log: boolean;
launch_url: string;
screenshots: {
enabled: boolean;
path: string;
on_failure: boolean;
};
desiredCapabilities: {
browserName: string;
};
webdriver: {
start_process: boolean;
server_path: string;
};
};
```

In the above test settings section, we can see the information being set about error logging:

- Default URL to be used for the application
- The browser name that we can set
- The server path and other information

The actual information which is available in the file is as follows:

```
test_settings: {
    default: {
        disable_error_log: false,
        launch_url: 'https://5elementslearning.dev/demosite/',
```

```
screenshots: {
  enabled: false,
  path: 'screens',
  on_failure: true
},

desiredCapabilities: {
  browserName: 'chrome'
},

webdriver: {
  start_process: true,
  server_path: ''
},

},
```

As we notice in the above test setting section, we have our default URL set to: **https://5elementslearning.dev/demosite/**, and the default browser set to **chrome**. For **chrome**, the settings available in the configuration file are:

```
chrome: {
    desiredCapabilities: {
      browserName: 'chrome',
      'goog:chromeOptions': {
        // More info on Chromedriver: https://sites.google.com/a/
chromium.org/chromedriver/
        //
        // w3c:false tells Chromedriver to run using the legacy JSONWire
protocol (not required in Chrome 78)
        w3c: true,
        args: [
          //'--no-sandbox',
          //'--ignore-certificate-errors',
          //'--allow-insecure-localhost',
          //'--headless'
        ]
      }
    }
```

In this section, we can notice that there are chrome browser settings available which we can set. So, with every instance of the browser getting launched, these settings can come into effect. For example, if we want to ignore certification errors, we can set the flag to true.

By making changes and adding information to the `nightwatch.conf.js` file, we can configure our test environment. Let us now have a look at the global variables.

Configuring the test global variables

Global variables are data points set at the configuration level so that the value associated with them can be used across test artifacts like test suites/test cases, etc. For example, we can have username and password set as global variables, just like the example in the `module_export` section. Additionally, Nightwatch also allows us to create a separate file where we can store all global variables, and then set its path in the configuration file. Either of these approaches are fine. We will discuss this in more detail in the upcoming chapters, as we get to designing the automation suite to be executed using Nightwatch.

Conclusion

In this chapter, we discussed different folders and files created when Nightwatch is installed in the system. We discussed the contents that are available in them, and how it is useful for us to use them to get started with writing our first test automation script. We had a look at nightwatch.conf.js and the configuration file, which helps us with the test environment configuration necessary for automation. We looked at its various sections, and what information they contain. We then looked at the default content, which was generated in the configuration file as we set up Nightwatch in the system.

In the next chapter, we will learn how to recognise web elements and automate our actions on them. It will bring us one step closer to writing our test scripts.

Questions

1. What are the two approaches Nightwatch provides to define global variables?

2. What does the folder page_object contain?

Answers

1. In Nightwatch, we can define global variables using two ways:

    a. Directly defining global variables in the configuration file.

    b. Creating them in a separate file and giving the path in the configuration file.

2. The default folder, which gets set when we install Nightwatch contains the page object information for the example script. It will also have the content that defines the web element of interest and how we can recognize the element using selector information.

Join our book's Discord space

Join the book's Discord Workspace for Latest updates, Offers, Tech happenings around the world, New Release and Sessions with the Authors:

https://discord.bpbonline.com

CHAPTER 4

Setting Visual Studio Code with Nightwatch

In the earlier chapter we saw the Nightwatch setup on the system and understood the various configuration files created. We saw what was contained in them and understood their explanation. Now, let us move to understanding how to set the system to ease the process of script generation and execution. Any good test development engineer requires a good interface to create, debug, and execute the scripts they are generating to automate web application testing they are working on. In this book, we will use Visual Code as the IDE for creating, debugging, and executing our scripts. This IDE has gained significant popularity in recent times. Nightwatch is available as an extension on this IDE. In this chapter, we will see how to set up Visual Code and the Nightwatch extension on the system and make it available as a ready environment to generate, debug, and execute the scripts.

Structure

In this chapter, we will discuss the following topics:

- Understanding Visual Studio Code
- Setting Visual Studio Code in system
- Adding the Nightwatch extension in the system
- Executing tests using the Nightwatch extension

Objectives

By the end of this chapter, you will be able to install and setup Visual Studio Code in the system and add the Nightwatch extension in the system. Further, you will be able to execute tests using the Nightwatch extension.

Understanding Visual Studio Code

Visual Studio Code is a source code editor, created by Microsoft. It runs on desktop and is available for operating systems like Windows, Linux, macOS. It has available built-in support for languages JavaScript, TypeScript, and Node.js. For other languages like Java, Python there are extensions available. It is a lightweight editor and has recently gained significant popularity.

More details on Visual Studio Code are available here: **https://code.visualstudio.com/**

Setting Visual Studio Code in system

To get started with Visual Studio Code, we need to install and set it up in our system. Once the source code editor is installed, we can proceed to the next step of getting the extension and executing tests of Nightwatch. To install and set up Visual Studio Code in the system, follow these steps:

Note: These steps are for Windows operating system.

1. Open the link **https://code.visualstudio.com/**, on a browser. You will find a section showing download Visual Studio Code, click on it, and download the appropriate version as per your operating system, as shown in the following figure:

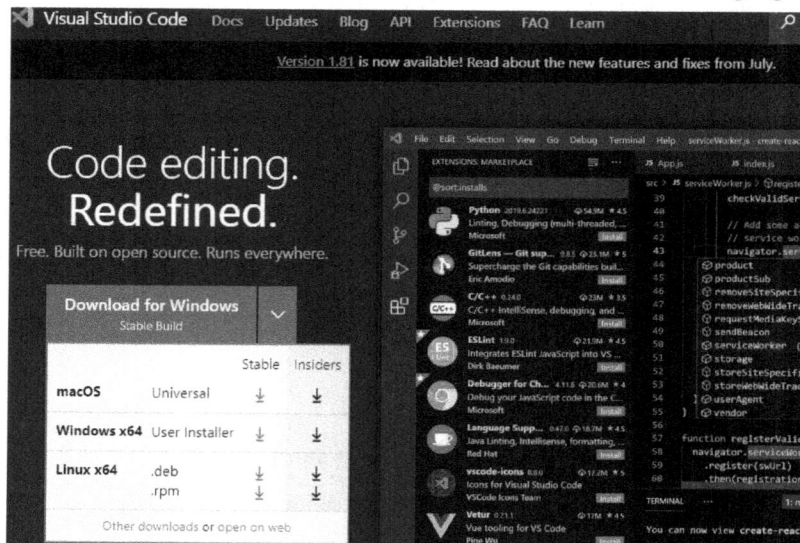

Figure 4.1: Finding the correct Visual Studio installer

2. Select the appropriate installer. For example, we will select for this book, Windows x64 stable installer. Once it is downloaded, we click on the installer to start the process by accepting the agreement, as shown in the following figure:

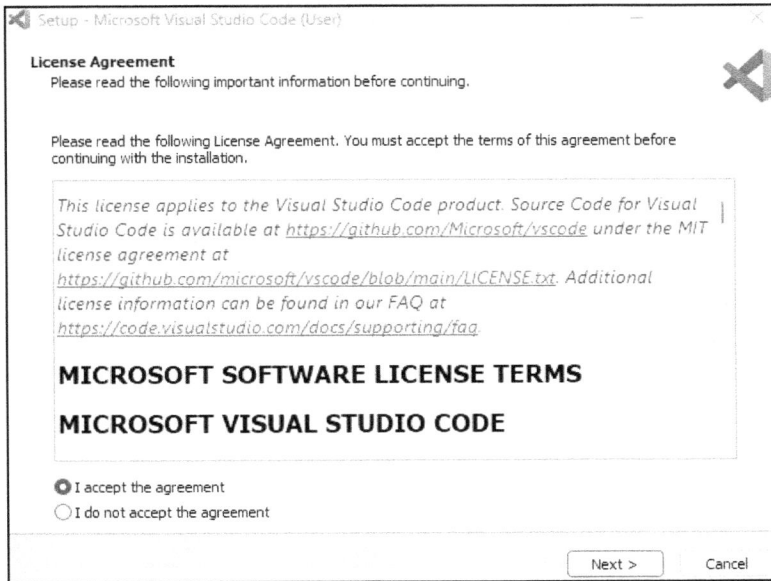

Figure 4.2: *Accept agreement to start Visual Studio Code installer*

3. Click on the next set of screens to reach the final installation screen. Select the **Install** button to proceed, as shown in the following figure:

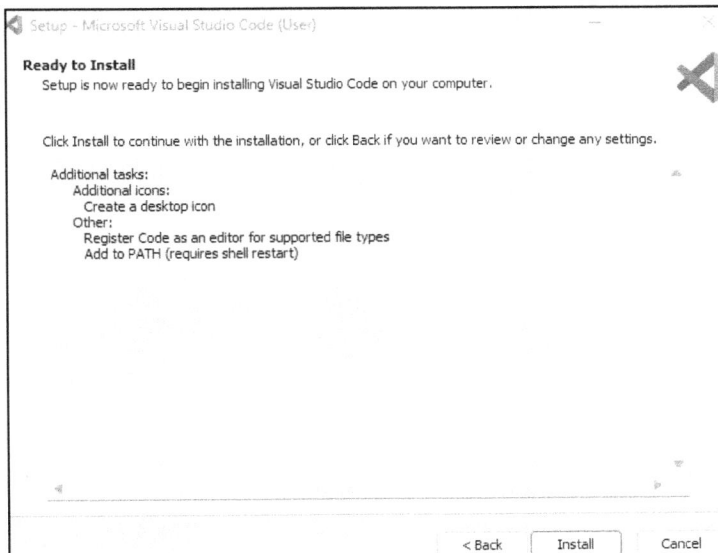

Figure 4.3: *Install Visual Studio Code*

4. Once the setup is complete, we will see the **Finish** button, and the option to **Launch Visual Studio Code**. Select that, as shown in the following figure:

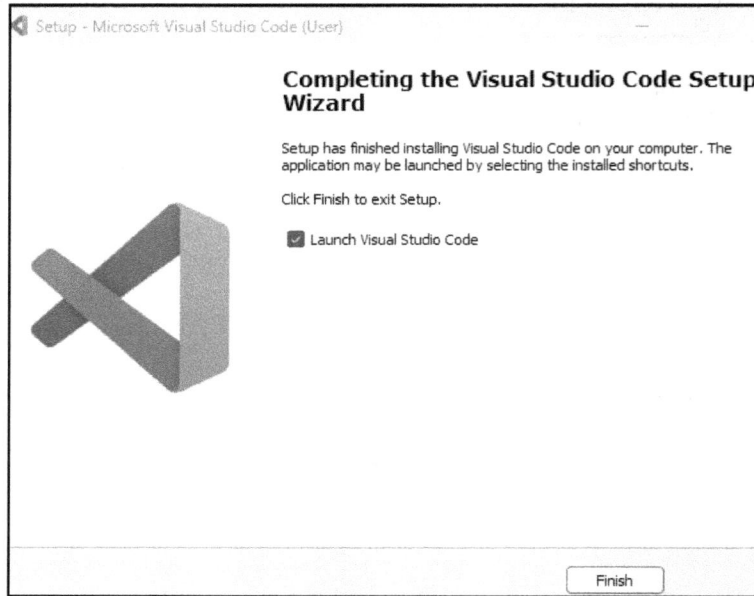

Figure 4.4: Launch Visual Studio Code

5. Once Visual Studio Code is set up and launched, we will see the following screen:

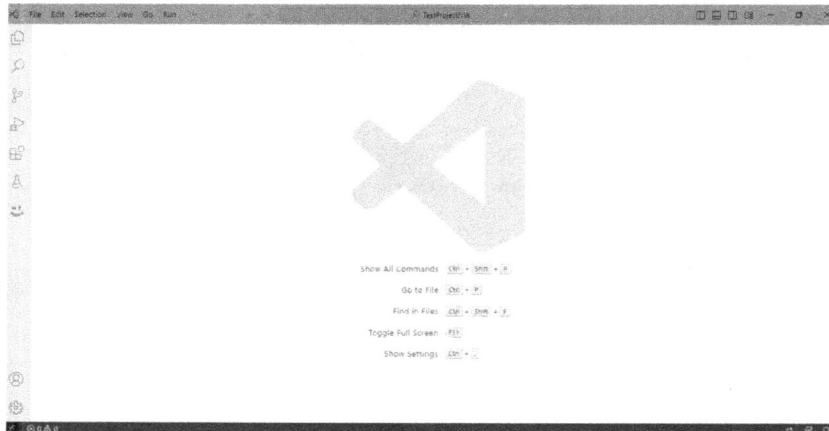

Figure 4.5: Visual Studio Code interface

6. Further, explore and open the project from the location which we provided when we configured Nightwatch, so that we can see all the example tests provided via the Nightwatch installer, and test their execution eventually. For this, select **File**, and **Open Folder** as shown in the following figure:

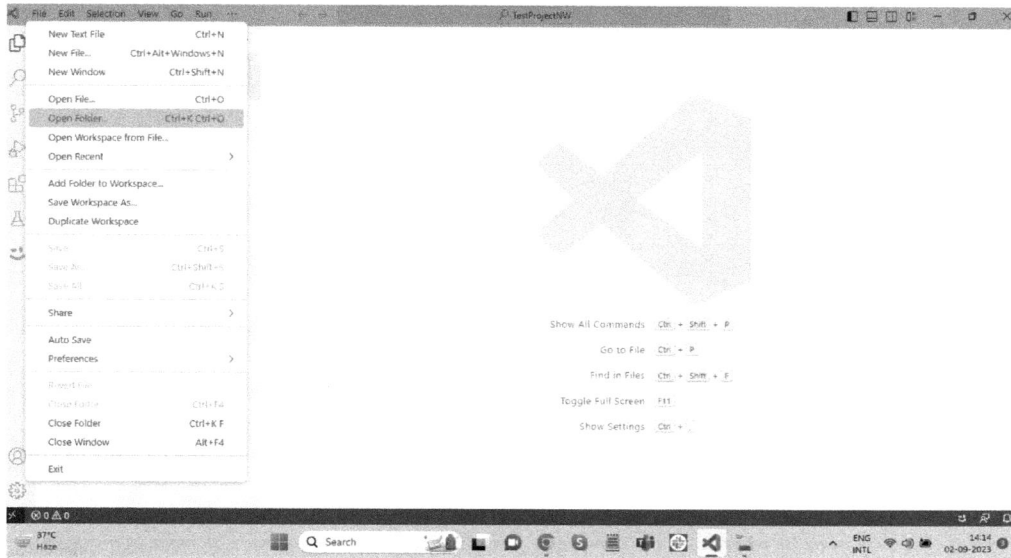

Figure 4.6: Open project folder

7. Go to the project **TestProjectNW**, select and open it in the explorer of Visual Studio Code, as shown in the following figure:

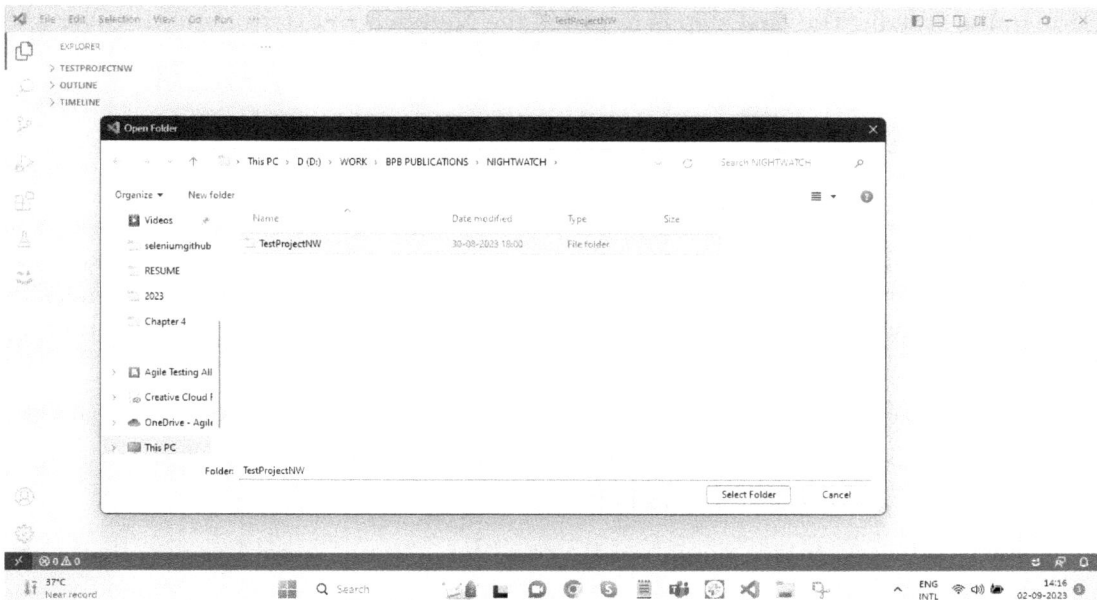

Figure 4.7: Open TestProjectNW

8. Once the folder is opened in the explorer, we can see the project contents and explore the files already available in it.

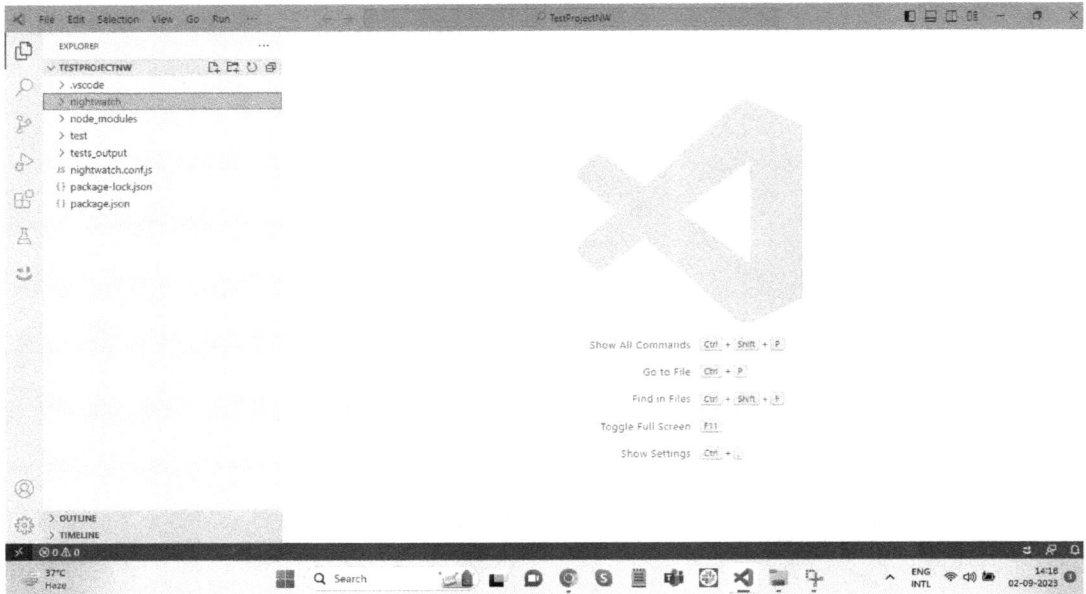

Figure 4.8: TestProjectNW folder contents

By following the preceding steps, we have successfully installed and set up Visual Studio Code in the system. The next step is to install the Nightwatch extension to discover and execute tests.

Adding the Nightwatch extension in the system

Once Visual Studio Code is installed, we can search for any extension from the marketplace depending on our requirements and availability. We can install these extensions to make the Visual Studio Code editor compatible with our requirements for test creation, debugging, and execution. Follow these steps to set the extension in the system:

1. Ensure you have already installed and setup Visual Studio Code in the system by following the above-mentioned steps.

2. Our next action is to visit this link:

    https://marketplace.visualstudio.com/items?itemName=browserstackcom. nightwatch.

3. Click on **Install** to set up the extension, as shown in the following figure:

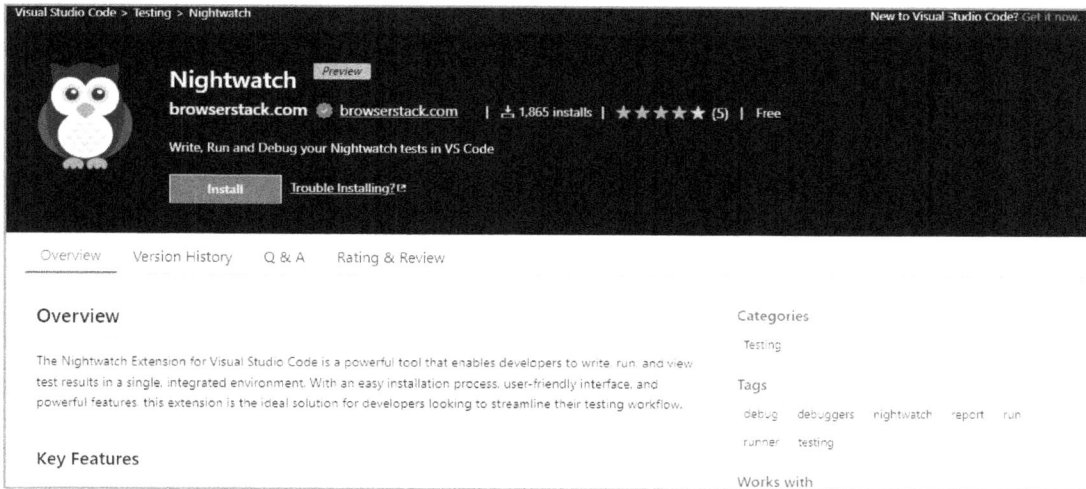

Figure 4.9: *Install Nightwatch as extension for Visual Studio Code editor*

4. Once we click on **Install**, it will ask us to open Visual Studio Code, which we will accept. The screen will look like the following:

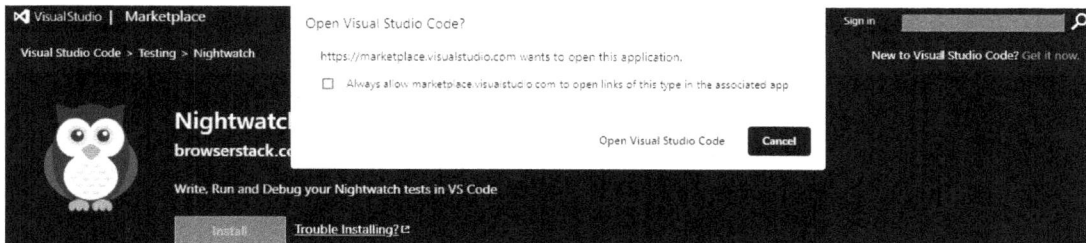

Figure 4.10: *Open Visual Studio Code for installation*

5. On selecting it, we will see the following screen in the Visual Studio Code editor, which now shows Nightwatch extension. Here, we will select the **Install** button and proceed.

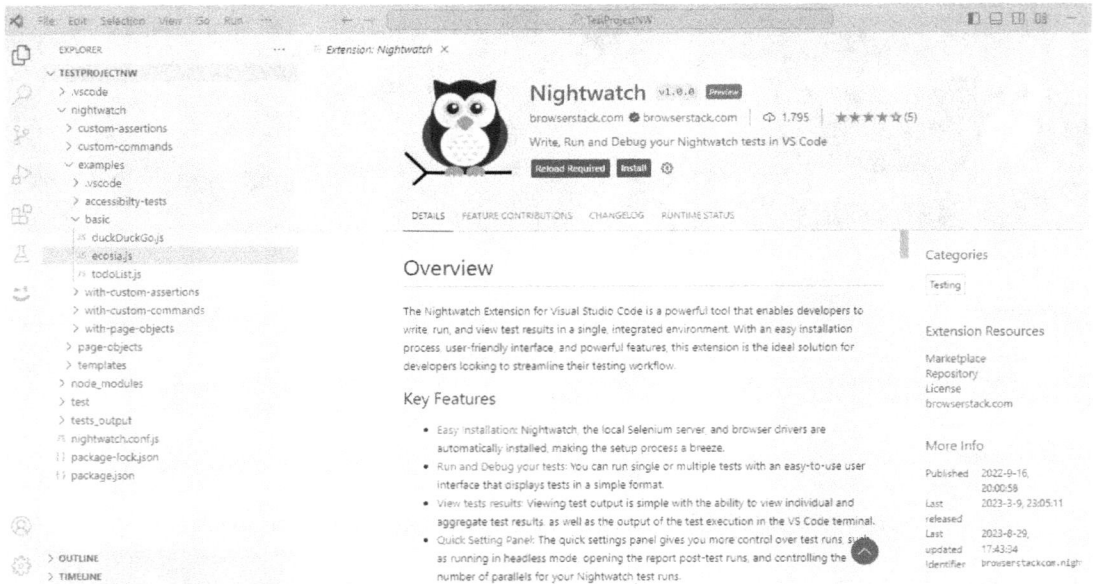

Figure 4.11: Install Nightwatch extension in Visual Studio Code

6. Once it is installed, we will see the message **This extension is installed globally**. We can now use Nightwatch Test Explorer to search for tests and execute them.

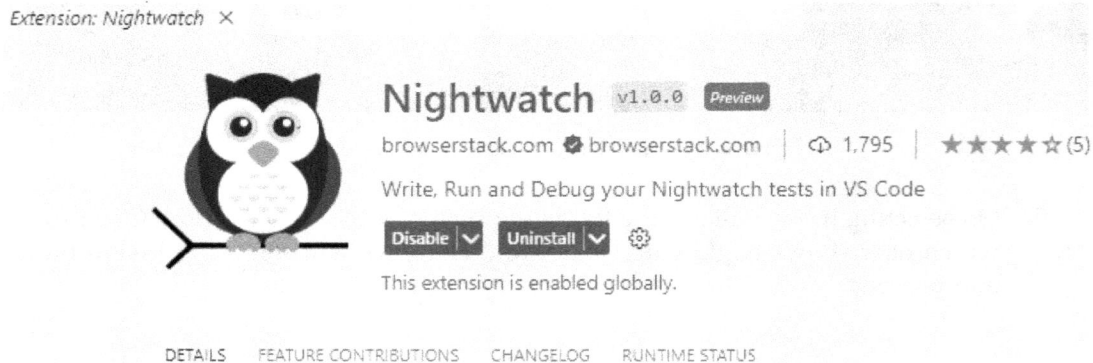

Figure 4.12: Nightwatch extension installed on Visual Studio Code editor

7. We can now click on the side panel, Testing icon, and it will show us Nightwatch quick settings, and Nightwatch environments tabs as shown in the following figure:

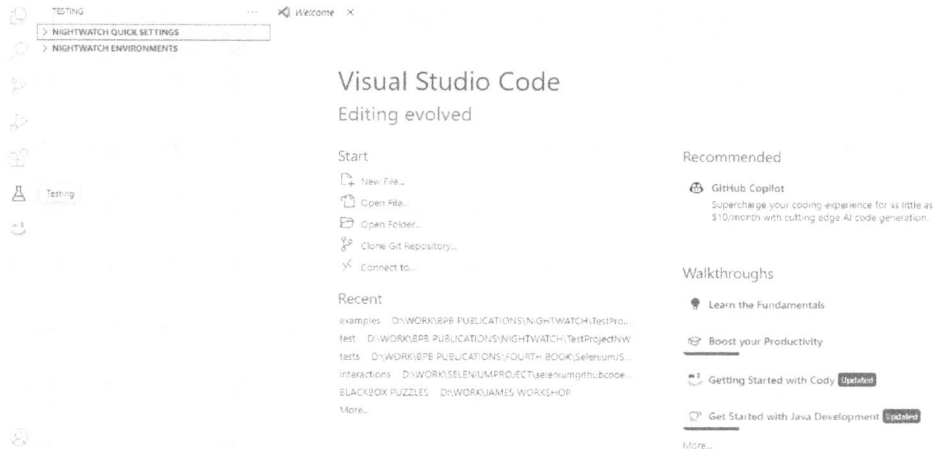

Figure 4.13: Nightwatch Test Explorer

With this, we have installed the Nightwatch extension in the Visual Studio Code editor. There could be more than one way to do this. Please explore the Visual Studio Code help section for it.

Executing tests using the Nightwatch extension

Now, as the environment is set, we can pick an existing example test from the project and execute it using the Nightwatch extension in the Visual Studio Code editor by following these steps:

1. The test selected for execution is in
   TestProjectNW\nightwatch\examples\basic\ecosia.js.

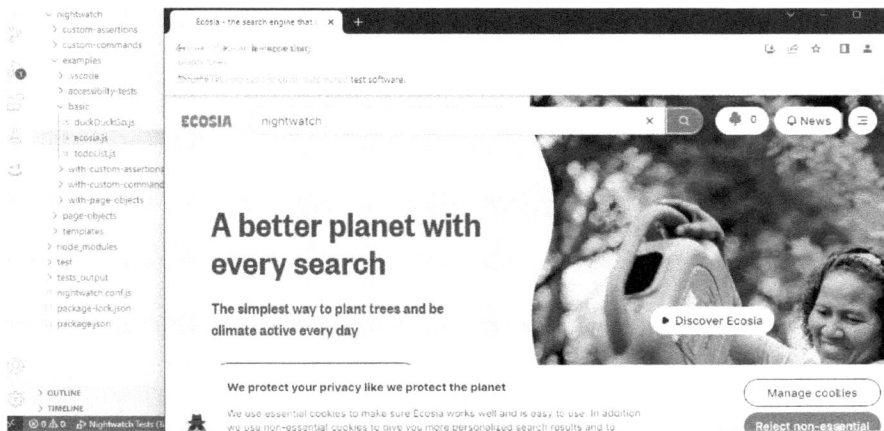

Figure 4.14: Test under execution

2. Once the test is executed, we can see the output of the execution in the debug console. It displays the assertion status which are passed, and the status of the execution, as shown in the following figure:

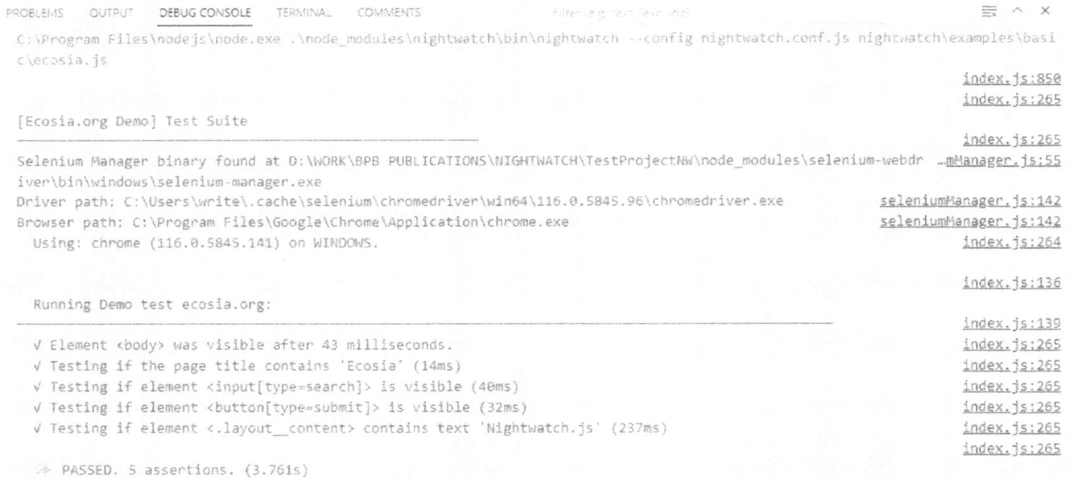

Figure 4.15: Test execution debug result

3. We can also explore the test result, available in the **TestProjectNW\test_output\ nightwatch-html-report** directory. The contents displayed are as follows:

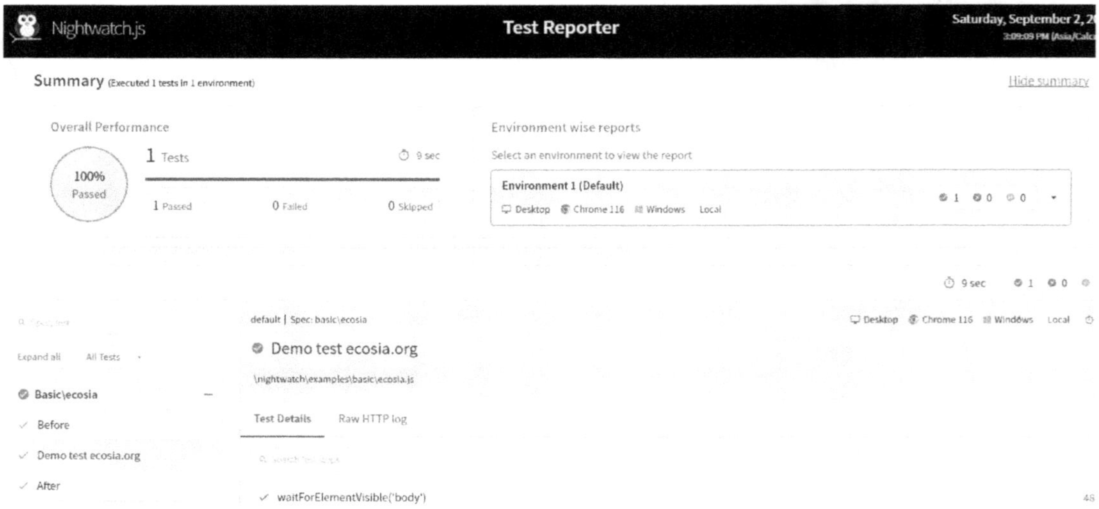

Figure 4.16: Test report after ecosia.js is executed using Nightwatch in Visual Studio Code

From the above steps, we have seen how to set Visual Studio Code in the system. After the Visual Studio Code editor is installed, we then saw how to install and set the Nightwatch extension. We then selected a file that came as an example file with Nightwatch installation and executed it in this environment. Finally, we saw the HTML report of the test after execution.

Conclusion

In this chapter, we understood the Visual Studio Code editor, and how it is useful for creating, debugging, and executing our test scripts, which we will write using JavaScript. This editor supports JavaScript, and Node.js by default. We saw how to setup this editor provided by Microsoft in the system. We then added extension of Nightwatch to this editor to make our test creation, debugging, and execution environment. Finally, we were able to execute an existing test and see the HTML report generated.

In the next chapter, we will learn to identify the web elements, understand their types, and learn about the different commands that can be used with them for automation.

Questions

1. What is Visual Studio Code?

2. Does it come with the Nightwatch extension?

Answers

1. Visual Studio Code is a source code editor provided by Microsoft.

2. By default, it does not come with the Nightwatch extension. We have to install it.

Join our book's Discord space

Join the book's Discord Workspace for Latest updates, Offers, Tech happenings around the world, New Release and Sessions with the Authors:

https://discord.bpbonline.com

CHAPTER 5
Identifying Elements

In the previous chapter, we discussed the configuration aspect of Nightwatch, looking at the various folders, and files structures which get created. We also saw the contents of the files and explained them in this chapter. As we move forward to understand how to use Nightwatch for automation of testing with web applications, an important concept is to understand how the tool identifies the web elements on the web page. Knowledge regarding the various ways elements can be recognized using Nightwatch, can help us write our scripts effectively. Let us learn about it in this chapter.

Structure

In this chapter, we will discuss the following topics:

- Understanding selectors
- Types of selectors in Nightwatch
- Understanding selectors from example web application
- Ways to locate web elements

Objectives

By the end of this chapter, you will be able to understand what selectors are and the different types of selectors available in Nightwatch. Further, you will understand, with examples, how to create selectors for web elements.

Understanding selectors

A web application is made of different web pages, and each web page has multiple web elements, which allow action to help achieve a business objective intended for the web page in the web application. As we create scripts to automate the testing of the web application, it becomes crucial to correctly identify the elements. Once the element is correctly identified, the command will act on it to complete the action. While understanding selectors, it also becomes crucial to understand which selector to use for an element. Not all types of selectors are advisable, as some may be more prone to changes, as the web application UI undergoes change. A selector is a way to find web elements on a web page by Nightwatch, so that the command can be executed on them.

Types of selectors in Nightwatch

The Nightwatch tool comes with its types of selectors, which we can use to identify the element. The following table shows what those selectors are:

S. no.	Selector name	Description
1.	CSS selectors	**Cascading style sheets** (**CSS**) are used in web pages for adding style to web elements. We can use the CSS selectors to identify web elements on the page.
2.	XPath selectors	A HTML document can be looked as an XML document, where we have root node, and nodes have a hierarchical relationship among them. When we then traverse the path to reach the element of interest, we call it the XPath, and we can use it as a selector to locate the element of interest.
3.	Text selectors	When we try to locate an element based on the Text displayed on the web page associated with it, we call it, Text based selector.
4.	Placeholder selector	A placeholder in the HTML acts as a hint for an expected value for an input field. We can use the text mentioned in placeholder as a selector to identify the web element.
5.	Alt text based	Many times, we come across web elements like images, links which have alt text associated with them. We can use these as selectors to identify the web element.
6.	Input based on labels	In a web page generally there exists, label as web elements. We can use these labels as selectors to identify the web elements.

S. no.	Selector name	Description
7.	Selecting nth element	Sometimes we can come across a set of web elements which share a common locator information. In this situation using that we can get a list of web elements. On that list we can use the nth element selector to find the web element of interest and work with it.

Table 5.1: Selectors in Nightwatch

In the above table, we saw the various selectors methods which are available in Nightwatch, how we can use them to identify the web elements. In the next section, we will discuss using all the above-listed selectors with an example web application.

Understanding selectors from example web application

To understand the selectors, we can create for web elements using the ones listed above, let us first look at the web application and the scenario we will use for it. We have discussed in detail this web application BPB Practice in *Chapter 2, Understand the Web Applications* used in the book. The URL of the web application is: **http://practice.bpbonline.com/**. The scenario we will be using to understand selectors will be the register user scenario. This is because it contains different kinds of web elements. This provides us with a good opportunity to create different selectors on different types of elements to automate the scenario. Before we do that, let us first see the scenario step by step:

1. Launch the application on a browser, using the URL: **http://practice.bpbonline.com/**. Refer to the following figure:

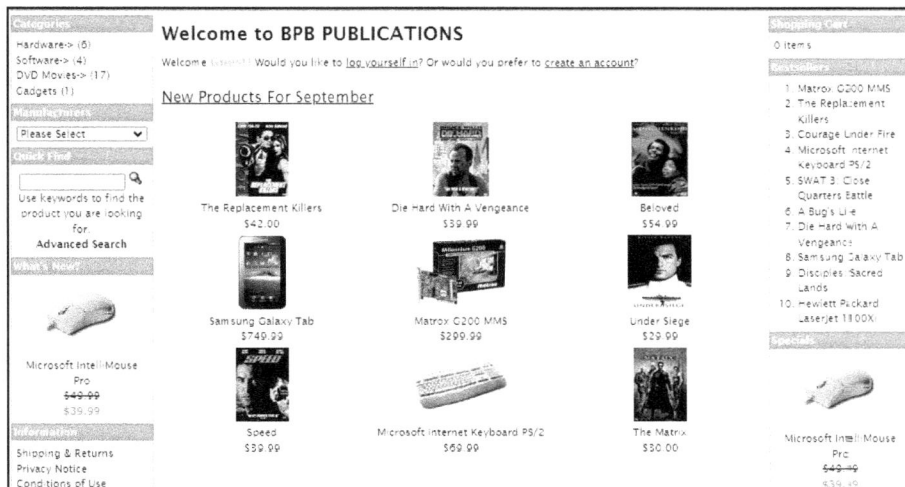

Figure 5.1: Home page of application

2. Click on **My Account** link, to go to the **Welcome**, **Please Sign In** page:

Figure 5.2: *My Account link*

3. In the next step, click on the **Continue** button of the **New Customer** section, to enter the **Register User** page, as shown in the following figure:

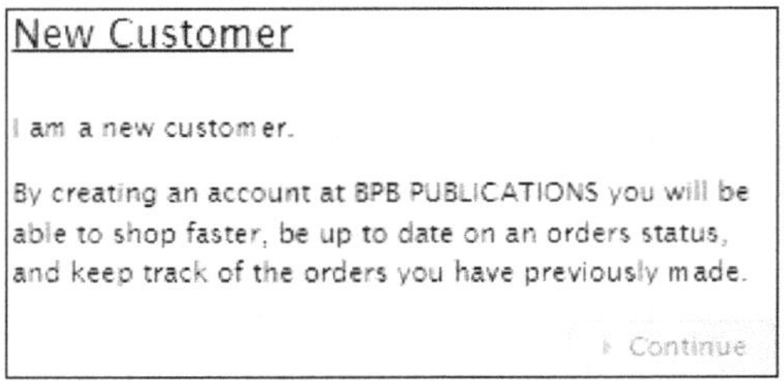

Figure 5.3: *Click on the Continue button of the New Customer section*

4. The **Register User** page will request information like **First Name**, **Last Name**, **Date of Birth**, **E-mail Address**, etc., to register a new user into the system, as shown in the following figure:

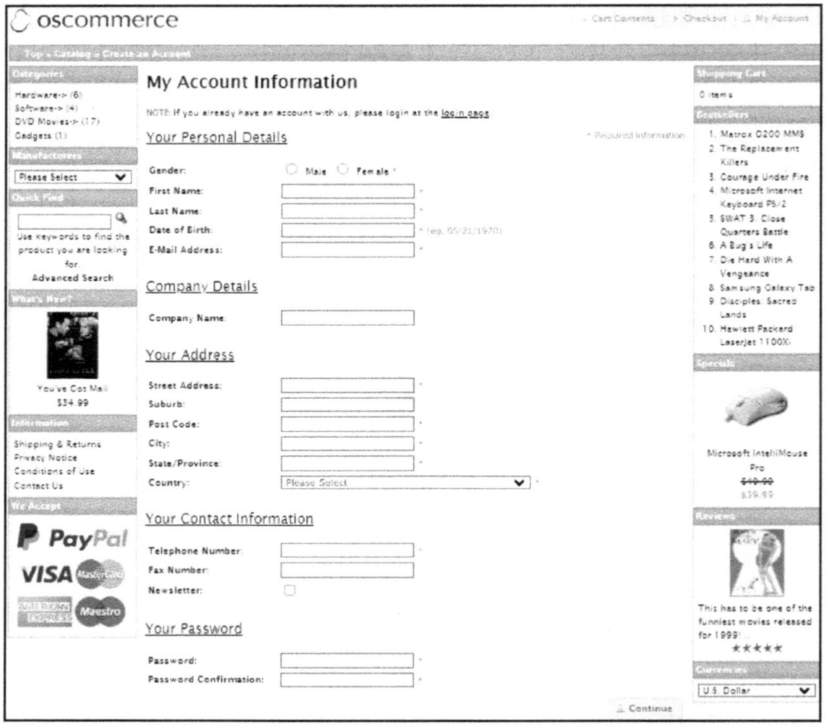

Figure 5.4: *Register user page*

5. We fill all the mandatory (*) fields in the page and then click on the **Continue** button. This will take us to the next page which mentions, **Your Account is Created**. Refer to the following figure:

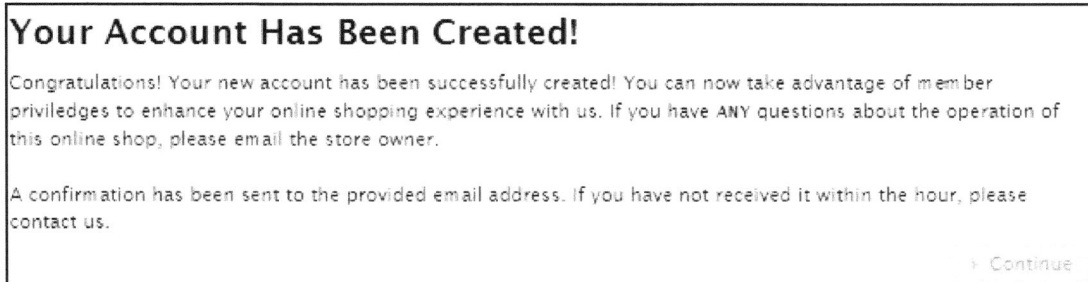

Your Account Has Been Created!

Congratulations! Your new account has been successfully created! You can now take advantage of member priviledges to enhance your online shopping experience with us. If you have ANY questions about the operation of this online shop, please email the store owner.

A confirmation has been sent to the provided email address. If you have not received it within the hour, please contact us.

› Continue

Figure 5.5: *Account Creation*

6. As we click on **Continue**, we will see the **My Account Information** page, where we can now proceed with changing account information, checking order history etc. Refer to the following figure:

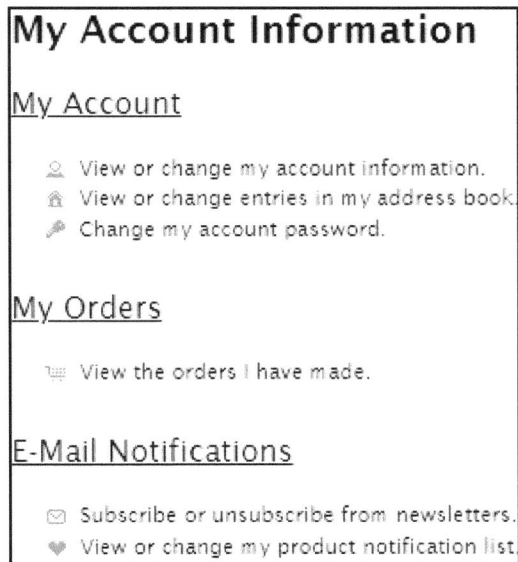

My Account Information

My Account

- View or change my account information.
- View or change entries in my address book.
- Change my account password.

My Orders

- View the orders I have made.

E-Mail Notifications

- Subscribe or unsubscribe from newsletters.
- View or change my product notification list.

Figure 5.6: *My Account Information*

7. In the next step, we click on the **Log Off** link and then click on the **Continue** to exit from the account created. Refer to the following figure:

Cart Contents   › Checkout   My Account   Log Off

Figure 5.7: *Log Off link*

8. Click on **Continue** to proceed with the complete exit. Refer to the following figure:

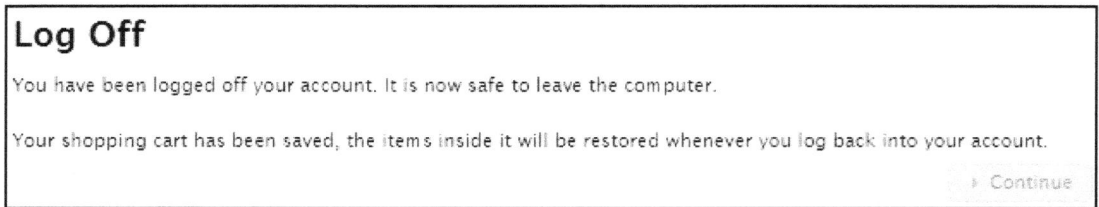

Log Off

You have been logged off your account. It is now safe to leave the computer.

Your shopping cart has been saved, the items inside it will be restored whenever you log back into your account.

› Continue

Figure 5.8: Continue to exit the account

Hence, as we perform the above steps, we can register the account for a new user.

Note: For logging in to the application, we will require the email address and password used while registering the user.

9. We will now list different web elements and the actions we need to perform. Next, we will add the selectors for these web elements. This will help us generate the test script.

The following table shows the web elements we will need and the action we have to perform on them:

S. No.	Web element	Type of web element	HTML information of the web element	Action on web element
1.	Gender(Female)	Radio button	`<input type="radio" name="gender" value="f">`	Click
2.	First Name	Text Box	`<input type="text" name="firstname">`	Type Text
3.	Last Name	Text box	`<input type="text" name="lastname">`	Type Text
4.	Date of Birth	Date Picker(custom class)	`<input type="text" name="dob" id="dob" class="hasDatepicker">`	Click
5.	Email Address	Text box	`<input type="text" name="email_ address">`	Type Text
6.	Street Address	Text box	`<input type="text" name="street_ address">`	Type Text
7.	Post Code	Text box	`<input type="text" name="postcode">`	Type Text
8.	City	Text box	`<input type="text" name="city">`	Type Text

9.	State	Text box	<input type="text" name="state">	Type Text
10.	Country	Drop down	<select name="country">..</ select>	Select Option
11.	Telephone	Text box	<input type="text" name="telephone">	Type Text
12.	Password	Text box	<input type="password" name="password" maxlength="40">	Type Text
13.	Confirm Password	Text box	<input type="password" name="confirmation" maxlength="40">	Type Text

Table 5.2: List of mandatory web elements for register user

We have listed information associated with the web elements, which we will have to use in the test script for registering the user. We have also listed the actions we will be performing on them. Now we will create selectors for these elements. Please note that it could be possible that there exists more than one selector for a web element. To cover all types of selectors available on Nightwatch we will show case the examples of them for the web elements we have from the register user.

The following table lists down the selectors for the web elements mentioned above:

S.No	Web element	HTML information of the web element	Type of selector used	Finding the web element
1.	Gender(Female)	<input type="radio" name="gender" value="m">	Selecting nth element	browser.element. findAll('radio').nth(2)
2.	First Name	<input type="text" name="firstname">	XPath selector	browser.element.find(by. xpath("//input[@ name='firstname']"))
3.	Last Name	<input type="text" name="lastname">	Input based on labels	browser.element. findByLabelText('Last Name:')
4.	Date Of Birth	<input type="text" name="dob" id="dob" class="hasDatepicker">	CSS selector	browser.element. find("#id")
5.	Email Address	<input type="text" name="email_ address">	XPath selector	browser.element.find(by. xpath("//input[@ name='email_address']"))

6.	Street Address	\<input type="text" name="street_ address"\>	CSS selector	browser.element. find("[name='street_ address']'")
7.	Post Code	\<input type="text" name="postcode"\>	Input based on labels	browser.element. findByLabelText('Post Code:")
8.	City	\<input type="text" name="city"\>	CSS selector	browser.element. find("[name='city']")
9.	State	\<input type="text" name="state"\>	CSS selector	browser.element. find("[name=state]'")
10.	Country	\<select name="country"\>..\</ select\>	XPath selector	browser.element.find(by. xpath("//select[@ name='country']"))
11.	Telephone	\<input type="text" name="telephone"\>	CSS selector	browser.element.find- ("[name='telephone']")
12.	Password	\<input type="password" name="password" maxlength="40"\>	CSS selector	browser.element.find- ("[name='password']")
13.	Confirm password	\<input type="password" name="confirmation" maxlength="40"\>	Input based on labels	browser.element.findByLa- belText('Password Confir- mation:")

Table 5.3: Selectors for web elements of register user scenario

The above table details out the selectors which can be created using the selectors available with Nightwatch, which are broadly classified as CSS selector or XPath selector. More information is available here: **https://nightwatchjs.org/guide/writing-tests/selectors. html**.

If not specified, the CSS Selector strategy is considered default by Nightwatch. We can change it by using the command **useXPath()** and if we wish to return to using CSS, we can use the command **useCss()**. Beyond the mentioned strategies we have some default element identification strategies which are available by default with WebDriver, on which Nightwatch is based. In the following section, let us have a look at them.

Ways to locate web elements

Besides the CSS and XPath selectors, we can also use the locators' strategies to identify the web elements on the page. Those locator strategies are listed in the following table:

S. No.	Locator	Description
1.	Link text	We can use the text displayed on the link to identify it. The keyword we use to create the selector us link text.
2.	Partial link text	We can use the partial text available with the link to identify it. The keyword which we can use to create the selector is— partial link text.
3.	Tag name	The tag name is the html tag associated with the web element, and it can be used to identify the web element.

Table 5.4: *Locators available other than XPath and CSS to identify web elements*

Hence, in the preceding table, we have listed the different locators available, which can be used to identify the web elements. We will take some example web elements and create locators using the strategies listed in the table above.

Creating locators of some example web elements

To help understand the usage of the mentioned locator strategies in helping find the element, we will take some examples from the BPB application. Follow these steps to know how to use locator strategies:

My Account link on the home page: **http://practice.bpbonline.com/**

1. We will create the locator for this web element using **link text** and **partial link text**. Refer to the following figure:

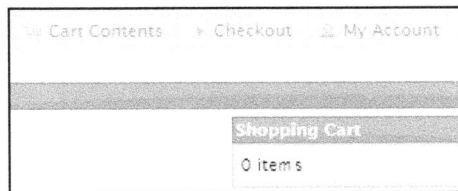

Figure 5.9: *My Account link*

Locator using link text - **'link text', 'My Account'**

Locator using partial link text - **'partial link text', 'Account'**

The Manufacturers select box on the home page: **http://practice.bpbonline.com/**

2. We will create the locator of this using **tag name**.

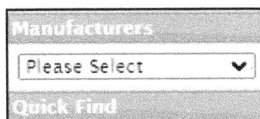

Figure 5.10: *Manufacturers select element*

3. Locator using **tag name** - **'tag name', 'select'**

Empowered with all the knowledge and information about creating selectors for web elements, now to help identify them, we will now create the script to register a user on this web application. Refer to the following code:

```
1.      describe('Register User BPB', function() {
2.          before(browser => browser.navigateTo('http://practice.
bpbonline.com/'));
3.          it('Register User BPB', function(browser) {
4.              browser
5.                  .useXpath() //setting locator to be used as xpath for
following commands
6.                  .click('link text', 'My Account') //click on My Account
Link
7.                  .click('link text', 'Continue') //click on Continue Link
8.                  .click("//input[@value='f']") //click female radio
button
9.                  .setValue("//input[@name='firstname']", "joey")//set first
name joey
10.                 .setValue("//input[@name='lastname']", "doey")//set last
name doey
11.                 .setValue("//input[@name='dob']", "12/01/1980")//set
date of birth
12.                 .setValue("//input[@name='email_address']", "joey5@doey.
com")//set email, remember to change this for every execution
13.                 .setValue("//input[@name='street_address']", "london
bridge")//set street address
14.                 .setValue("//input[@name='postcode']", "312431")//set
post code
15.                 .setValue("//input[@name='city']", "london")//set city
16.                 .setValue("//input[@name='state']", "london")//set state
17.                 .setValue("//select[@name='country']", "United
Kingdom")//set country
18.                 .setValue("//input[@name='telephone']", "831248103")//
set telephone
19.                 .setValue("//input[@name='password']", "joeydoey")//set
password
20.                 .setValue("//input[@name='confirmation']", "joeydoey")//
set confirm password
21.                 .click("//button[@id='tdb4']")//click on Continue button
```

```
22.              .click('link text', 'Continue')//click on Continue Link
23.              .click('link text', 'Log Off')// Click on Log Off Link
24.              .click('link text', 'Continue')//Click on Continue to
Log off
25.          });
26.      after(browser => browser.end());
27.    });
```

This code will register a user to the BPB application. Please note we have not used any assertion of an action in the above script for simplification. Hence, the preceding code example is not a test script but a script to register a user, which we can execute using Nightwatch.

Conclusion

In this chapter, we discussed what selectors are and how we can use them to identify the web elements on the web page. After identifying the web element, we can then perform action on it. We saw the selectors and created them for a scenario of registering the user for the BPB application. We also saw other web element locating strategies that are available besides using XPath and CSS selectors. We finally created a script to perform the actions using Nightwatch.

In the next chapter, we will learn how to interact with the web elements.

Questions

1. What are selectors used for in Nightwatch?

2. What is the purpose of the command useXPath()?

Answers

1. In Nightwatch, selectors identify the web elements in the web application so that the action can be performed on them.

2. The purpose of the command useXPath() is to set the context that now for all commands following it, the default selector strategy to locate an element will be XPath. By default, Nightwatch uses CSS.

Join our book's Discord space

Join the book's Discord Workspace for Latest updates, Offers, Tech happenings around the world, New Release and Sessions with the Authors:

https://discord.bpbonline.com

CHAPTER 6
Interacting with Web Elements

In the previous chapter, we learned how to identify a web element on the page. We explored the various ways to locate a web element on Nightwatch. We understood that these are called **locators**. We also created locators to identify the different types of web elements in the scenario of user registration from the BPB application. In this chapter, we will explore the different types of commands Nightwatch provides us with to interact with the Web Elements. These commands help us execute actions on the web elements, which help us generate the script to automate our actions. Let us further read about how we can interact with the web elements and the different types of commands Nightwatch provides us with.

Structure

In this chapter, we will discuss the following topics:

- Importance of interacting with web elements
- Types of interactions

Objectives

By the end of this chapter, you will be able to understand why we need to interact with web elements. Additionally, you will understand the different types of available interactions.

Importance of interacting with web elements

A web page is made up of web elements. In the previous chapter, we understood how to identify the web element on which we want to perform an action using locators. After the web element is identified, we have to interact with the web element, in the same manner as an end user will do to complete a scenario to achieve a business objective. For example, on a text box, an end user would want to type text or clear information. If there is a link, an end user would want to perform a click action on it so that it can take it to the next page. Interacting with the web elements is a required prerequisite. In the next section, we will learn about the types of interactions that are available.

Types of interactions

We know that a web page is made up of different types of web elements. For example, a text box, a link, an image, a drop down, a web table, and so on. We are also aware of the fact that we perform different actions on these web elements as an end user to complete a scenario. We would want to open an application first, then maybe click on a link, fill the information in a text box, select an option from the drop-down, and then click on the submit button. To verify our actions, we might also need to fetch information from the web elements and validate it against an expected result. We have the following types of interactions:

- Performing an action on a web element.
- Fetching information from a web element.
- Updating a web element.

We will first understand the functions available to perform actions on the web element. Through that action, an event must happen on the application, which changes its state. The following table is where we will list out the actions, what they do, and the type of web elements they act on:

S. No.	Command	Web element/s	Details
1.	SendKeys	Input elements like TextBox	This action sends keys to the input element. For example, we want to type text in a textbox.
2.	Click	Web elements like button, link, image	This will perform a click action on the web element. For example, clicking on a link will take us to the next page.
3.	Double click	Web elements like button, link, image	This will perform a double click action on the web element.

4.	Right click	Context menu	The right click mouse action generally is used to display context menu. Hence, when performed on a web element on the page, a context menu appears.
5.	Clear	Input web elements like text box	This action will clear the contents of the web element, for example, we want to clear content of a text field before typing a new one.
6.	Set value	Input web elements like text box	This action will set the value of the input field.

Table 6.1: Action commands from Nightwatch

In the preceding table, we have discussed different commands that are available to perform actions on the web elements. In the next section, we will discuss the available commands that will help us fetch the state of the web element. Generally, this helps us in building validations for our actions as we create test scripts using Nightwatch. The following table displays details about the different commands available that help in getting information from web elements:

S. No.	Command	Web element	Details
1.	Get text	Web element	This command will fetch the text associated with the web element.
2.	Get value	Web element like a text box	This command will fetch the typed contents of the text box.
3.	Get tag name	Any web element	This command will fetch the html tag name associated with the web element.
4.	Get attribute	Any web element	This command will fetch the data associated with the attribute of the web element.
5.	Get CSS property	Any web element	This command will fetch the CSS details associated with the web element.
6.	Get ID	Any web element	This command will fetch the id information associated with the web element.
7.	Get accessibility name	Any web element	This command will fetch the WAI-ARIA label of an element (related to accessibility).
8.	Get rect	Any web element	This command will fetch the Rect (height and width) of an element.

Table 6.2: Get commands from Nightwatch

In the previous table, we had a look at the commands that help us fetch information associated with a web element. In the next section, we will have a look at the commands which will help us to update the web element as required. Let us have a look at the following table for the commands associated with it:

S. No.	Command	Web element	Details
1.	Set text	Any web element	This command will set the text associated with the web element.
2.	Set attribute	Any web element	This command will set the attribute of the html property, associated with the web element.
3	Set geolocation	Any web element	This command sets the latitude and longitude at the browser level. This helps us to simulate traffic.

Table 6.3: Set Commands from Nightwatch

As we have looked at the commands mentioned above, which will help us interact with the web elements, we will now create a script where we will be using these functions. We will take the login logout scenario from the BPB web application. Let us have a look at the scenario steps first:

1. Open the application using the URL: **https://practice.bpbonline.com/**

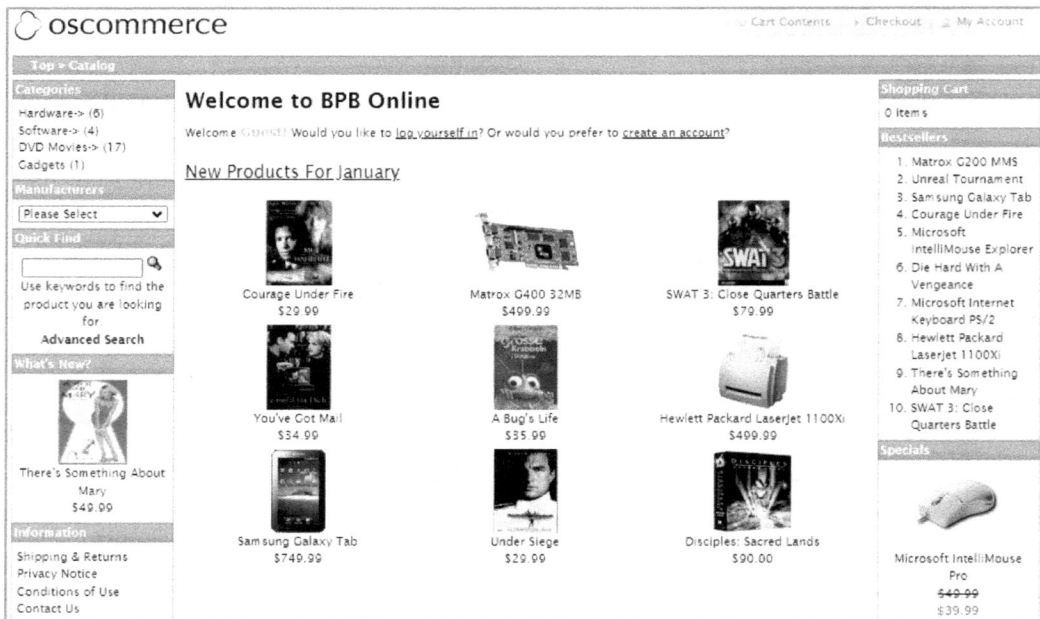

Figure 6.1: Home page of the application

2. Click on the **My Account** link to reach the **Sign in** page:

Figure 6.2: *My Account link*

3. On the **Sign in** page, provide the credentials of the registered user, to log in to the application. Provide both username, and password and click on the **Sign In** button, as shown in the following figure:

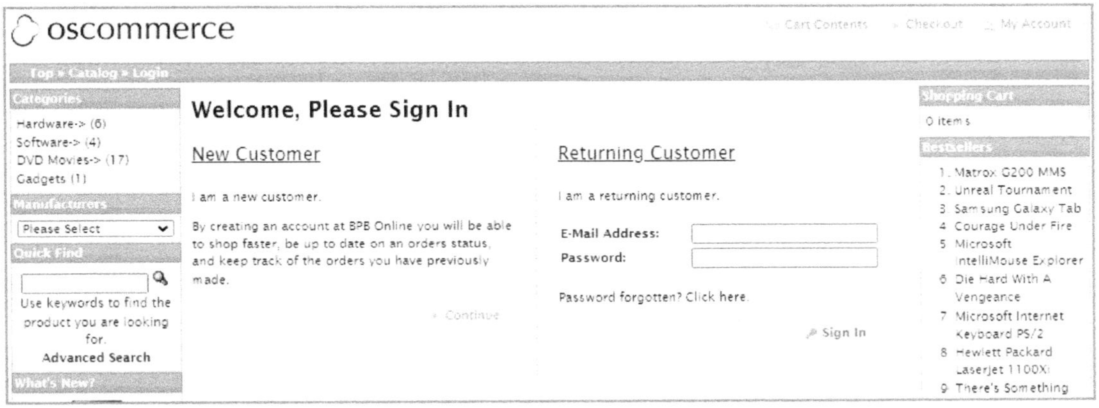

Figure 6.3: *Sign in page of application*

4. Once you have logged in, you will see the **My Account Information** page as follows:

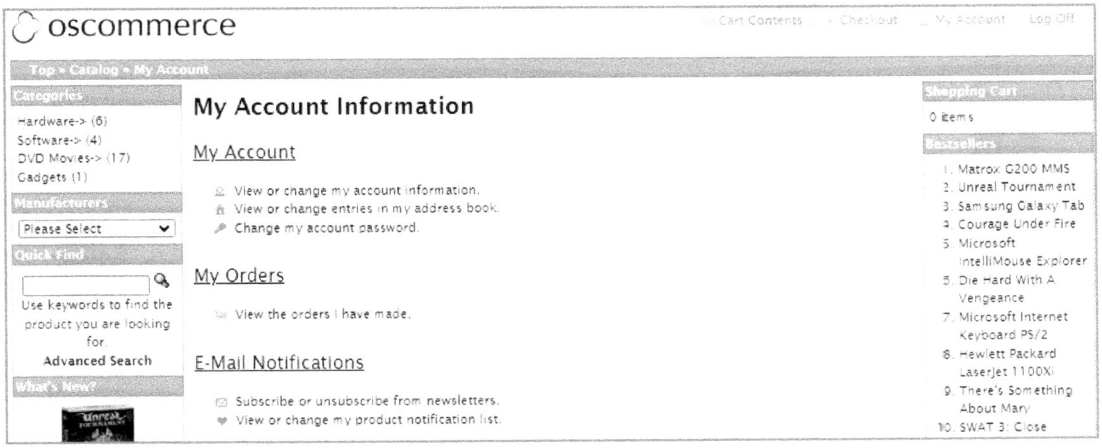

Figure 6.4: *My Account Information page*

5. Once you have logged into the application, you can see information related to your account, like password changes, orders made, etc. You can now also see the **Log Off** link, which we will click to log out from the application, as shown in the following figure:

Figure 6.5: Log Off link

6. Once you click on **Log Off**, you will see the log off page, and a button, displaying **Continue**. Clicking on continue will complete the logging out action. Refer to the following figure:

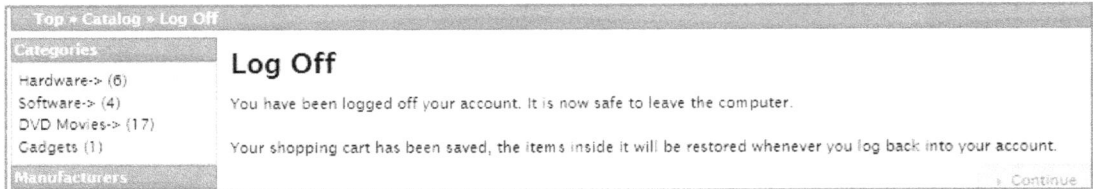

Figure 6.6: Log Off page

7. Clicking continue will take us back to the home page of the application, as shown in the following figure:

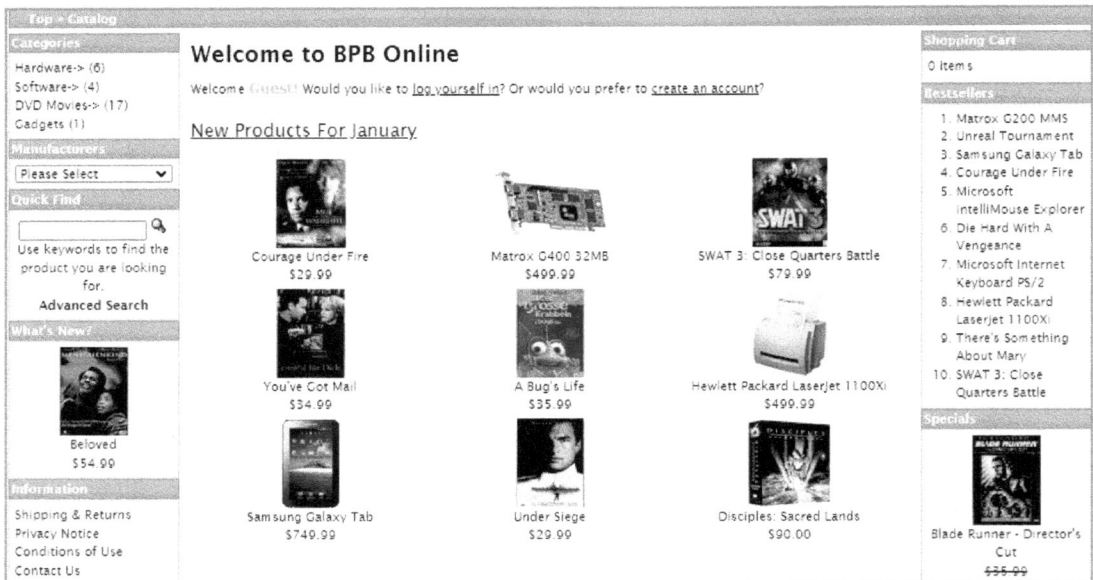

Figure 6.7: Home page of application

As we can see in the preceding steps, to perform the login-logout action on the application, we will have to interact with different web elements. We came across the links we clicked, textboxes in which we typed text, and the buttons that were clicked to go to the next page. Hence, a user flow is completed by interacting with the different web elements on the page. Now, let us look at the script which we will write using commands from Nightwatch to perform the login-logout on the application. Refer to the following code:

```
1.      describe('Login Logout BPB', function() {
2.          before(browser => browser.navigateTo('http://practice.
   bpbonline.com/'));
3.          it('Register User BPB', function(browser) {
4.              browser
5.                  .useXpath() //setting locator to be used as xpath for
   following commands
6.                  .click('link text', 'My Account') //click on My
   Account link
7.                  .setValue("//input[@name='email_address']", "bpb@bpb.
   com")//set email
8.                  .setValue("//input[@name='password']", "bpb@123")//set
   password
9.                  .click("//button[@id='tdb5']")//click on Sign in
   button
10.                 .click('link text', 'Log Off')//click on Log Off link
11.                 .click('link text', 'Continue')// Click on Continue
   Link
12.             });
13.         after(browser => browser.end());
14.     });
```

This code we just looked at performs the login logout on the application by interacting with the different web elements on different web pages of the application. We first identify the web elements based on the locator. Once the element is uniquely located, the action will be performed on them. Let us look at an example command:

browser.click('link text', 'My Account')

In this command, we take the instance of the browser, on which the URL of the application is launched, and perform the click action on the link which is identified by its display text: My Account. Similarly, all other commands should be inferred as mentioned in the code.

The following table shows the web elements, the locators used to identify them, and the action we performed on them to achieve the login and logout of the application:

S no	Web element	Locator	Action	Comment
1.	My account	Link text— My Account	Click	On the My Account link perform the click action.
2.	Email address	name-email_ address	Send keys	Type text bpb@bpb.com on the text box which will be recognised using the name property—email_address.

S no	Web element	Locator	Action	Comment
3.	Password	name-password	Send keys	Type text bpb@123 on the text box which will be recognised by the name property—password.
4.	Sign In	id-tdb5	Click	Perform Click on the Sign In button.
5.	Log Off	Link text—log off	Click	Perform click action on the link identified using the link text Log Off
6.	Continue	Link text—continue	Click	Perform click action on the link identified using the link text Continue.

Table 6.4: Web elements and the commands from the login logout scenario

In the same way, we can automate other scenarios from the application. We need to first identify the web elements that we encounter in the business flow. We then need to identify the locator associated with them and perform appropriate action on them to achieve the automation of the scenario using Nightwatch.

Conclusion

In this chapter, we discussed what interactions are, and the different types of interactions available with different web elements. We saw an end-to-end business scenario of login and logout in the application and wrote the script to automate it. We first had to identify the web elements in the login logout scenario, then use the appropriate action, and thus, we were able to automate it using Nightwatch.

In the next chapter, we will discuss the concept of synchronization.

Questions

1. If we have to fetch the data displayed in a text field, what command will we use?

2. Where is the set geolocation command helpful?

Answers

1. To fetch the data displayed in the text field, we will need to use the Get Attribute command. The attribute will be value.

2. The Set geolocation command helps us set the latitude and longitude. This helps in simulating network traffic for a geographic location.

CHAPTER 7
Synchronization

In the previous chapter, we learned how to interact with different web elements using different actions, which helps complete a user action on the web page. As the script gets executed by the tool in discussion here, we need to match the speed of executing the command sent by the tool to the web page to the speed of the web page executing the command in time before it receives another command. This can be done by a concept very common in automation called synchronization. It means, as the word says, to happen at the same time. We need this to be in place in the automation script for tests, so that the errors do not come because of it. In Nightwatch, synchronization is inbuilt. Let us understand that in this chapter.

Structure

In this chapter, we will discuss the following topics:

- Importance of synchronization in automation
- Nightwatch and applying synchronization
- Concept of command queue
- Concept of callback function in Nightwatch
- Understand the order of command execution in Nightwatch
- Commands for wait in Nightwatch

Objectives

By the end of this chapter, you will understand the importance of synchronization for test scripts created for automation. You will also learn how Nightwatch applies synchronization, the concept of command queue, and the callback function in Nightwatch. You will also understand the order of command execution in Nightwatch, and the command wait to be used in Nightwatch.

Importance of synchronization in automation

Synchronization means two or more activities happening at the same rate. As we design our automation test scripts, to automate the process of web application testing using any tool, it is crucial that we take into consideration the need for synchronization. When a test script executes, it sends the command to the web application. The web application, in turn, performs the action and comes to a state to accept the next request by executing the test script. If the script sends a command without caring about the state of the application, as in whether the application was able to execute the command, was it ready to handle the upcoming request? If this is not taken care of by the test script, then we will start facing errors.

For example, let us take a scenario where we click on a link, which takes us to a new page. On the new page, we have to enter some text in a text field. Now, as the script is executing, it has sent the command to the web application for link click, the application is processing it, and starts loading the new page. However, before the page load is completed and the text field web element is visible, the test script sends the next command for entering text. This will cause failure since the element is not visible or available on which the next command is to be executed. If we had implemented synchronization, the script, before sending the next command would have waited for the page to load, and only then sent the command to enter text in the text field. Now, the question arises, how much wait will be a good wait. After all, we do not want the automated test script to take more time for execution than a human would. Hence, a fine balance is required to understand how much wait should be applied for synchronization.

Nightwatch and applying synchronization

Nightwatch is built using JavaScript, which is an asynchronous language. This means we do not have to wait for the response to a command we sent for execution. This could become an issue in having synchronization in place. Since it is important for scripts written for automation to have the execution code in order, Nightwatch came up with a concept of a command queue, which we will have a look at in a bit. Nightwatch still allows you to use the vanilla state of JavaScript. In case you are doing that, you can use—*async* and *await* commands together. To understand this better, let us look at *callback hell* and *Promise*.

Other programming languages like Java, C#, and Python have the concept that when one line of code is executed entirely it allows execution of the next line of code. This is not true for Javascript since it allows us to create async functions or functions that use callback to execute and provide results later. This creates callback hell, largely when code is written in top to bottom order. To understand more, read about it in detail here: **http://callbackhell. com/**

To overcome *callback hell*, JavaScript came up with the concept of *Promise*. A *Promise* assures that a result will be returned for the asynchronous function. A Promise could be in one of the three states—pending, fulfilled, or rejected. This becomes a tad bit complicated for a developer to manage, and work with. To know more about Promise in JavaScript, read about: **https://developer.mozilla.org/en-US/docs/Web/JavaScript/Reference/Global_ Objects/Promise**

As mentioned, Nightwatch does allow us to use async and await, if we wish to use it. With this in mind, let us try to understand what command queue is in Nightwatch and how it works to help us with synchronization for our test scripts.

Concept of command queue

To overcome the problems associated with JavaScript, Nightwatch uses the command queue. When we write a script for the test in Nightwatch, it creates a command queue. It is a list in which the commands are added using the **first in first out** (**FIFO**) concept. This means the command that was written first will get executed, and only after it the next command will get executed. This is very helpful and required for Web UI test execution.

Before we proceed further to understand command queue, we need to understand that every Nightwatch command is a wrapper command for underlying Selenium Command, or to be specific WebDriver API command. This means when we call a *click* command in Nighwatch, it is a wrapper around the click command of Selenium, and to be precise, the WebDriver API. To know more about WebDriver API, **https://www.w3.org/TR/ webdriver2/**. Let us revisit the figure we saw in *Chapter 1, Introduction to Nightwatch,* describing the same:

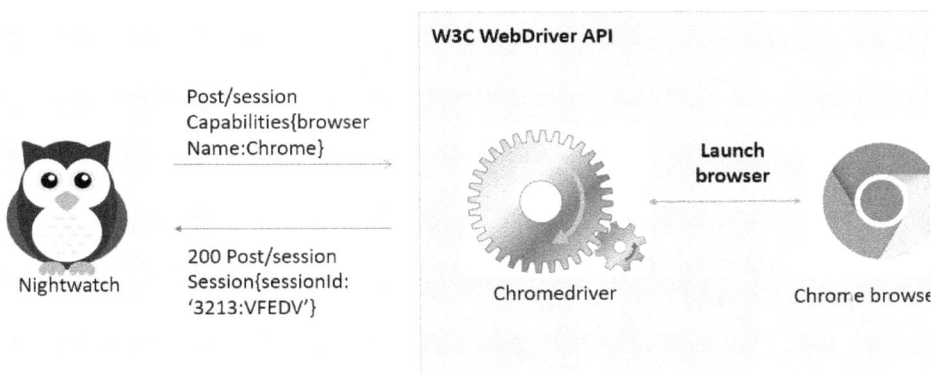

Figure 7.1: Command execution of NightWatch

If you are unaware of Selenium, it is a very popular, open-source web browser automation solution. Nightwatch is built over Selenium to extend its web browser automation capabilities for testing purposes using JavaScript specifically. To know more about Selenium, visit this link: **https://www.selenium.dev/**.

So, when we send a test script to be executed by Nightwatch, it resolves the command and store them in the command queue synchronously. Once the commands are stored, the queue is traversed, and the commands are called in asynchronous mode for execution of the scenario. Let us see an example of a test script and the command queue that will be generated for it by Nightwatch.

For understanding the command queue, let us take the example of the login logout scenario from the BPB application: **http://practice.bpbonline.com/**. The steps are as follows:

Launch the application with the URL: **http://practice.bpbonline.com/**

1. Click on the **My Account** link:

Figure 7.2: My Account link

2. Type in an existing user, email address in the **E-mail Address** text field. Further, type the **Password**, in the password field and click on the **Sign In** button, as shown in the following figure:

Figure 7.3: Log In section

3. Once the credentials for the existing user are filled, and sign in is clicked, we see the **My Account Information** page.

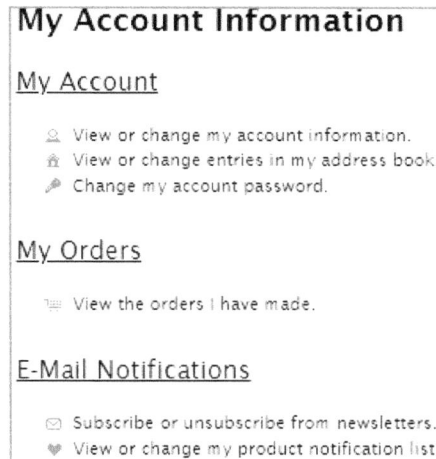

Figure 7.4: *My Account page*

4. The next step would be to proceed to log out. Click on the **Log Off** link on the page, as shown in the following figure:

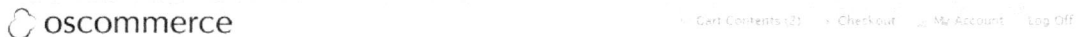

Figure 7.5: *Log Off link*

5. We then click on the **Continue** button to complete the **Log Off** action, as shown in the following figure:

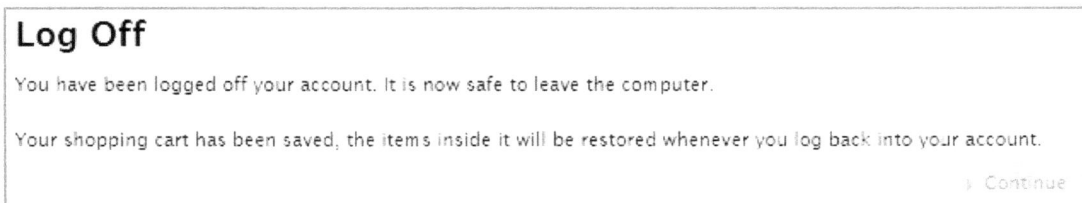

Figure 7.6: *Continue link*

6. We will now be back to the home page of the application.

Let us now take a look at the script we will need to write to perform these steps. Please note that the following is a script, not a test script, as it does not contain any steps to verify the actions we have performed on the web application. Once we learn about assertion in the coming chapters, we will understand how to design a test script:

```
1.    describe('Login Logout BPB For command queue Demo', function() {
2.        before(browser => browser.navigateTo('http://practice.bpbonline.
      com/'));
3.        it('Register User BPB', function(browser) {
```

```
4.          browser
5.             .useXpath() //setting Locator to be used as xpath for
    following commands
6.             .click('link text', 'My Account') //click on My Account Link
7.             .setValue("//input[@name='email_address']", "bpb@bpb.com")//
    set email
8.             .setValue("//input[@name='password']", "bpb@123")//set
    password
9.             .click("//button[@id='tdb5']")//click on Sign in button
10.            .click('link text', 'Log Off')//click on Log Off Link
11.            .click('link text', 'Continue')// Click on Continue Link
12.        });
13.      after(browser => browser.end());
14.    });
```

Let us look at the command queue which will get generated:

```
[
  {command: 'navigateTo', args: ['http://practice.bpbonline.com/']},
  {command: 'useXPath', args: []},
  {command: 'click', args: ['link text', 'My Account']}
   {command: 'setValue', args: ["//input[@name='email_address']", "bpb@bpb.
com"]},
  {command: 'setValue'', args: ["//input[@name='password']", "bpb@123"]},
  {command: 'click', args: ["//button[@id='tdb5']"]},
  {command: 'click', args: [''link text', 'Log Off'']},
  {command: 'click', args: ['link text', 'Continue']},
  {command: 'click', args: ['button']},
  {command: 'end', args: []}
]
```

As we notice in the above command queue generated for the Nightwatch commands, all the commands are put in FIFO order. These commands will now be executed in asynchronous mode. There is a small catch here, which we will learn in the next section, talking more about call back, command queue and execution. If you wish to read more on command queue visit this link: **https://github.com/nightwatchjs/nightwatch/wiki/Understanding-the-Command-Queue**

Concept of callback function in Nightwatch

In the above section of this chapter, we have discussed **callback hell**, and the need for the command queue to execute scripts by Nightwatch. Now, let us understand callback.

As per the MDN Web Document (**https://developer.mozilla.org/en-US/docs/Glossary/Callback_function**), a **callback** function is passed into another function as an argument. It is then invoked in the outer function to complete an action. For example, let us have a look at the following code:

```
1.    // function
2.    function sayHello(name, callback) {
3.        console.log('Hello' + ' ' + name);
4.        callback();
5.    }
6.
7.    // callback function
8.    function callMe() {
9.        console.log('callback function');
10.   }
11.
12.   // passing function as an argument
13.   sayHello('Diana', callMe);
```

The output of the above would be as follows:

Hello Diana

callback function

First, the lines of the **sayHello** function will get executed which will print **Diana**, and then the function **callMe()** will be called, which then prints the **callback function** in the output window. The callback function is used by the Nightwatch tool. Before we understand the deeper reason behind this, we need to explore another interesting aspect of how Nightwatch commands are built over the WebDriver protocol.

The Nightwatch commands are of two basic types:

- **Protocol commands**: These commands are used for one-to-one mapping of the W3C WebDriver Protocol. For example, **url** command, this navigates to the URL of the application passed.

- **Composite commands**: These commands chain two or three W3C WebDriver commands and create one command. For example, **isVisible**.

For the application of the composite commands, as different methods are chained one after the other, Nightwatch cannot provide a return value. So, Nightwatch uses a **callback** function that can be processed to provide a return value if required. To understand more, let us look at the **isVisible** command here: **https://nightwatchjs.org/api/isVisible.html**

```
.isVisible(selector, [callback])
.isVisible(using, selector, [callback])
```

To see its usage and the **callback** value, let us write a small script:

```
1.    describe('isVisible Command Execution Demo', function() {
2.        before(browser => browser.navigateTo('http://practice.bpbonline.
      com/'));
3.        it('isVisible Function', function(browser) {
4.            browser
5.                .useXpath() //setting locator to be used as xpath for
      following commands
6.                .click('link text', 'My Account') //click on My Account link
7.                .isVisible("//button[@id='tdb5']",response => console.
      log(response))//check if Sign in button is visible
8.
9.            });
10.       after(browser => browser.end());
11.    });
```

We will find in console logs following printed after execution of the script:

```
                    Running isVisible Function:
                    _____

                  > {value: true, status: 0}
```

Figure 7.7: *Output of isVisible command*

So, the command will execute and check, if the Sign in button is visible, it will print its response which we requested in the callback function. As we can see from *Figure 7.7*, it is **true**, which means that the element is visible. If required, we can store this response and use it further for decision-making, or assertion activity for the scenario we want to test. Through this above example, it should now be clear how Nightwatch is using callback function for its methods. More details can be explored from this link: **https://nightwatchjs. org/api/commands/#getValue**

With the understanding of what is command queue in Nightwatch, and how Nightwatch commands are written using method chaining, where and how callbacks are then used by Nightwatch, let us try to understand the code execution order for a script written in Nightwatch in the next section.

Understand the order of command execution in Nightwatch

Unlike code written for synchronizing script execution with application behavior, we need to be careful when applying these concepts of wait in Nightwatch. Due to callbacks, and command queue, it is crucial that we are clear with the order of execution of commands written in the script, and how the application will receive these commands for execution. For any script execution that happens in Nightwatch, the command queue is created for Nightwatch commands. However, if there is any JavaScript command in the code, they will be executed first. So the order of execution will be as follows:

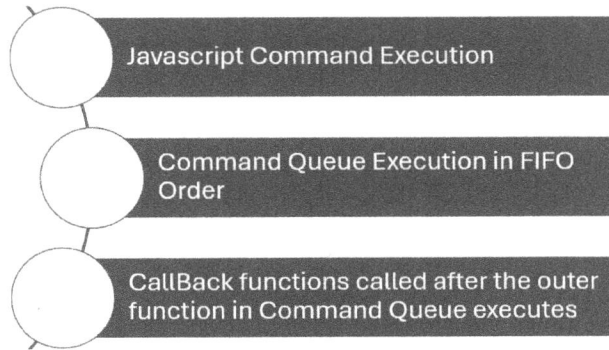

Figure 7.8: Command execution flow of script in Nightwatch

Let us take an example to understand this. The steps will be:

1. Launch the browser with the URL of the application: **https://practice.bpbonline.com/**

2. Type in a search text—we are using Nightwatch as text, as shown in the following figure:

Figure 7.9: Search field in application

3. We then get the value of text, entered in the field—store it in a variable and print on console.

4. In the next line, we simply print anything on the console.

The script is as follows:

```
1.    describe('Command queue Demo', function() {
2.        before(browser => browser.navigateTo('http://practice.bpbonline.
      com/'));
3.            it('Nightwatch Command Execution Flow', function(browser) {
```

```
4.              .browser
5.                .useXpath() //setting locator to be used as xpath for
      following commands
6.                  .setValue("//input[@name='keywords']", "Nightwatch")
7.                  .getValue("//input[@name='keywords']", ({ value }) =>
      console.log("call back command: "+value))
8.                  .clearValue("//input[@name='keywords']") // clears input
      field
9.               console.log('direct javascript command');
10.              });
11.         after(browser => browser.end());
12.       });
```

If we are used to programming languages like Java or C#, we will assume that the first thing that will get printed in the console is Nightwatch. Then it will print—**direct javascript command**. However, since this is written in JavaScript and commands are executed using Nightwatch, the console logs get printed as follows:

```
Running Nightwatch Command Execution Flow:
─────────────────────────────────────────────
direct javascript command
```

***Figure 7.10**: Output of the script*

As we see the above output, it should become clear to us that the first command the Nightwatch will execute is the one written in JavaScript:

```
console.log('direct javascript command');
```

Then, it will execute commands in FIFO order as created in command queue. So, as per the command queue, when it comes to the following command: **.getValue("//input[@ name='keywords']", ({ value }) => console.log("call back command: "+value))**, it will first execute the **getValue** command, and then the callback of the command, which stores the text content fetched into the **value** field, and then prints on the console.

Commands for wait in Nightwatch

Understanding how Nightwatch executes commands was crucial to now explore the wait commands available. For effective synchronization to be added at the script level, sometimes we will require help of the wait commands. This will ensure that the speed at which the script is sending commands for execution, as well as the order, is the same which is being followed by the application, whose scenario we are automating. Let us look at the commands available with Nightwatch which will help us introduce wait:

1. `waitUntil()`
2. `waitForElementVisible()`
3. `waitForElementNotVisible()`
4. `waitForElementPresent()`
5. `waitForElementNotPresent()`
6. `pause()`

These commands can help introduce wait in Nightwatch script, which can benefit with synchronization. Let us look at these commands.

waitUntil()

This command waits for an event to happen for a given timeout. The default timeout is 5000 milliseconds. If the event does not happen and timeout occurs, we get a failure message; else, if the action is successful, whatever message we have passed in the command will get printed. The syntax of this command is:

`.waitUntil(action, {timeout, retryInterval, message, abortOnFailure});`

If the action does not happen and timeout occurs, the current script execution will halt. We can change this by setting **abortOnFailure** to -false. The following script shows the usage of the command. The steps which we will take are as follows:

Launch the application using URL, **http://practice.bpbonline.com/**

1. Wait for the My Account link, to be visible. Here, we will give a bad locator to identify the element, to cause script failure. This is done to check for wait action to happen. So, we will pass the locator as the find element using the text: **'My Account Demo'**. However, this does not exist. The script is as follows:

```
1.    describe('waitUntil() Command', function() {
2.      before(browser => browser.navigateTo('http://practice.
    bpbonline.com/'));
3.      it('waitUntil() command', function(browser) {
4.        browser
5.          // with xpath as the locate strategy
6.          .element.find(by.linkText('My Account Demo')).
    waitUntil('visible', {message: 'My Account link is found'})
7.          .click('link text', 'My Account') //click on My Account
    link
8.
9.        });
10.     after(browser => browser.end());
11.   });
```

2. As mentioned, we are waiting until the link with text **'My Account Demo'**, becomes visible. This command will go into failure after the default timeout of 5000ms happens. On execution, you will find a slight delay, which is where the wait is acting and then the following failure message:

```
- waitUntil() command (7.407s)

→ ✕ NightwatchAssertError
My Account link is found - expected "visible" but got: "not visible" (2071ms)

- OTHER ERRORS:
Error
  Error
  Timed out while waiting for element "By(link text, My Account Demo)" to be present for 5000 milliseconds.
```

Figure 7.11: Output of waitUntil on failure

3. Now, if we use the same script with correct locator information for the element, we will see the following happening:

```
1.    describe('waitUntil() Command', function() {
2.      before(browser => browser.navigateTo('http://practice.
      bpbonline.com/'));
3.      it('waitUntil() command', function(browser) {
4.        browser
5.          // with xpath as the locate strategy
6.          .element.find(by.linkText('My Account')).waitUntil('visible',
      {message: 'My Account link is found'})
7.          .click('link text', 'My Account') //click on My Account
      link
8.
9.        });
10.     after(browser => browser.end());
11.   });
```

4. This time, since we have passed the correct locator, the script will execute successfully. The output will be as follows:

```
Running waitUntil() command:
─────────────────────────────────

√ My Account link is found

✓ PASSED. 1 assertions. (907ms)
```

Figure 7.12: waitUntil() success message

If you wish to learn more about this command, visit the link: **https://nightwatchjs.org/api/element/waitUntil.html**

waitForElementVisible() and waitForElementNotVisible()

In this section, we will look at the commands `waitForElementVisible()`, and `waitForElementNotVisible`. These commands wait for an element to be visible. The default timeout is 5000 milliseconds. If the element appears within the wait, the command passes, and the script moves to the next step for the execution. If not, then the script execution aborts with a failure message. The syntax of the command is:

`.waitForElementVisible([using], selector, [timeout], [pollInterval], [abortOnAssertionFailure], [callback], [message]);`

The other command waits for the default timeout of 5000 milliseconds for the element to be not visible. This command can be used in a scenario where some action causes an element to be deleted. If the element is not visible within the default timeout, the script passes; otherwise, it fails. The syntax for the command is:

`.waitForElementNotVisible([using], selector, [timeout], [pollInterval], [abortOnAssertionFailure], [callback], [message]);`

We will take the following scenario, where we wait for a popup to appear, if it appears, we click on the **Ok** button. If, after pressing **Ok**, the alert disappears, then the script execution will be successful, which means we will wait for the element not to be visible. Let us look at the following steps, which we will automate:

Launch the application with the URL:

https://the-internet.herokuapp.com/add_remove_elements/

Add/Remove Elements

Add Element

Figure 7.13: Add/Remove Element

1. We click on **Add Element**. This creates another element on the page: **Delete**. Here, we use the `waitForElementVisible()` function to wait for the element **Delete** to appear on the page, as shown in the following figure:

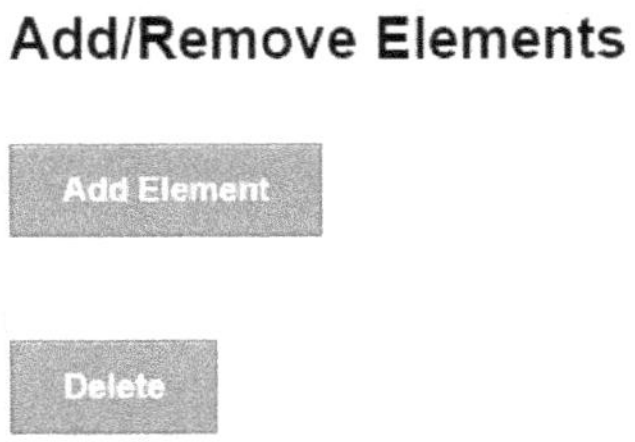

Add/Remove Elements

Add Element

Delete

Figure 7.14: Delete Element

2. We now click on the **Delete** element. This will take the page back to its original state. Let us see the script:

```
1.   describe('waitForElementVisibleFunctions Command', function() {
2.     before(browser => browser.navigateTo('https://the-internet.
   herokuapp.com/add_remove_elements/'));
3.     it('waitForElementVisibleFunctions', function(browser) {
4.       browser
5.         // with xpath as the locate strategy
6.         .useXpath() //setting locator to be used as xpath for
   following commands
7.         .pause(2000) //command given to see execution
8.         .click("//*[contains(text(), 'Add Element')]") //click on
   Add Element
9.         .waitForElementVisible("//*[contains(text(), 'Delete')]")
   //wait for Delete button to become visible
10.        .click("//*[contains(text(), 'Delete')]") //click on
   Delete Element
11.        .pause(2000) //command given to see execution, can be
   removed
12.        .waitForElementNotVisible("//*[contains(text(),
   'Delete')]",10000,"This element is deleted")
13.        //Wait for Delete Button to be not be not visible, with a
   timeout of 10 seconds
14.      });
15.    after(browser => browser.end());
16.  });
```

3. As we execute the above script, you will find the application adding an element, and then deleting it. The script passes with the following message:

```
Running waitForElement command:

√ Element <//*[contains(text(), 'Delete')]> was visible after 33 milliseconds.
√ This element is deleted

  PASSED. 2 assertions. (4.193s)
```

Figure 7.15: Output of waitforelementvisible functions execution

To learn more about these commands, the following links are helpful:

https://nightwatchjs.org/api/waitForElementVisible.html

https://nightwatchjs.org/api/waitForElementNotVisible.html

In the above script, we will also see the usage of **.pause()** function. The purpose of **pause** function is to halt or pause the execution for the number of milliseconds pass into it as an argument. This is sometimes helpful in script synchronization, acting as a static or forced wait. Sometimes, this command is also helpful for debugging purposes. The reason this command is used here in the script is to create a brief pause where the end user can see the commands working on the application; otherwise, the actual execution is fast enough for a human eye to make sense. This, once understood, can be easily removed from the script. To read more about the **pause** function, visit the link: **https://nightwatchjs.org/api/pause.html**

waitForElementPresent() and waitForElementNotPresent()

The commands **waitForElementPresent()**, introduce the wait in the script until the element appears, or timeout happens. In the similar manner, **waitForElementNotPresent()** waits for the default time period of 5000 milliseconds for the element be present in the application or not. It will pass if the element is not present. It will cause script failure if the element is available within the wait time mentioned.

To understand its working, we will perform the following actions:

1. Launch the application with the URL:

   https://the-internet.herokuapp.com/forgot_password

Figure 7.16: Forgot password application for demo

2. We will use **waitForElementPresent**, for the **Retrieve password** button. If this function passes, we will then click it.

3. We will again use the **waitForElementNotPresent**, for the same button. This will cause our script to fail. To avoid failure, we will set the **abortOnAssertionFailure** flag of the function as false, so the message will get printed, but the script execution will not fail.

4. To showcase that the execution will continue even after assertion failure, we click on the Retrieve password button, which will take us to an internal server error page. This is the behavior of the application.

Figure 7.17: Page after clicking retrieve password button

Let us see the script:

```
1.    describe('waitForElementPresentFunctions Command', function() {
2.      before(browser => browser.navigateTo('https://the-internet.
herokuapp.com/forgot_password'));
3.      it('waitForElementPresentFunctions', function(browser) {
4.        browser
5.          // with xpath as the locate strategy
6.          .useXpath() //setting locator to be used as xpath for
following commands
7.          .waitForElementPresent("//*[contains(text(), 'Retrieve
password')]","Retrieve Password is Present")
8.          //wait for element to be present
9.          .pause(2000) //command given to see execution, can be removed
10.         .waitForElementNotPresent("//*[contains(text(), 'Retrieve
password')]",1000,false,"Retrieve Password is not absent")
11.         //wait for element to be not present
12.         .click("//*[contains(text(), 'Retrieve password')]")
13.         //deliberately clicking on the button to show, that execution
is allowed as the flag set to false.
14.         .pause(2000) //command given to see execution, can be removed
15.       });
16.     after(browser => browser.end());
17.   });
```

As we execute the script, we will see the following output, where we see an assertion failure being reported, which is expected, but the script still executes:

```
FAILED: 1 assertions failed and  1 passed (5.11s)


TEST FAILURE (10.327s):
 - 1 assertions failed; 1 passed

 ⨯ 1) codeexamplesbook\chapter7-waitForElementPresent

 - waitForElementPresentFunctions (5.11s)

 → ⨯ NightwatchAssertError
 Retrieve Password is not absent - expected "not found" but got: "found" (1049ms)
```

Figure 7.18: Assertion failure

To know more about these functions, visit these links:

https://nightwatchjs.org/api/waitForElementPresent.html

https://nightwatchjs.org/api/waitForElementNotPresent.html

Thus, with understanding the availability and usage of the wait commands, we can synchronize our scripts with the execution on the application.

Conclusion

In this chapter, we learned about the importance of synchronization. We understood how Nightwatch uses concepts like the command queue to set the execution. We understood the concept of callback and callback hell. Finally, with this, we were able to understand and see with an example, the wait commands that can help make better synchronized scripts.

In the next chapter, we will learn about using assertions in Nightwatch. This will help us verify our actions, thus allowing us to convert our scripts into test scenarios.

Questions

1. What is command queue?

2. What is callback hell?

3. What are the different wait commands available in Nightwatch?

Answers

1. Command queue is a FIFO mechanism used by Nightwatch to set the order of execution of commands mentioned in the script.

2. Callback hell is a scenario which gets created in JavaScript program execution, when multiple call backs are listed inside each other, thus causing difficult to manage the code execution flow.

3. The different wait commands available in Nightwatch are waitForElementPresent(), waitForElementNotPresent(), waitForElementVisible(), waitForElementNotVisible(), waitUntil() and pause().

Join our book's Discord space

Join the book's Discord Workspace for Latest updates, Offers, Tech happenings around the world, New Release and Sessions with the Authors:

https://discord.bpbonline.com

CHAPTER 8

Assertions in Nightwatch

In the previous chapter, we learned how to use synchronization to ensure that our scripts run reliably when automating the application. We understood how Nightwatch commands help us achieve that. In this chapter, we will talk about another crucial concept of assertions. For any script that we write, our context to write that script is to automate the browser for the user actions for test purposes. Any actions that are conducted need to be verified; only then can we call it a test. So, the actions we conduct, when asserted or verified, confirm whether the scenario we are trying to automate has passed or failed. This helps in assessing the health of the underlying application in tests.

Nightwatch has a list of commands that fall under the umbrella of assert and expect. In this chapter, we will look at what those commands are and how we can use them in our scripts to convert them into test scripts.

Structure

In this chapter, we will discuss the following topics:

- Introduction to assertions
- Assertions in Nightwatch
- Using assertions in script
- Understanding expect
- Using expect in script

Objectives

After completing this chapter, you will be able to understand assertions, and assertion commands available in Nightwatch and script. Further, you will be able to understand expect in Nightwatch, and how it helps in verifying actions. By the end of this chapter, you will also learn to use *expect* in scripts.

Introduction to assertions

Assertions are code statements that we add to our script to verify the action we are performing. Verification of the action is necessary to ensure the completion of the test case. Based on whether the test case has passed or failed, we can identify the health of the underlying application and communicate with the stakeholders about the state of the system being developed.

In tools like Selenium, which is a browser automation tool, built-in assertions are not available. Rather, if we want to use assertions in the script, we will have to add a *unit test framework* based on the programming language we are using. Those unit test frameworks provide us with libraries with different assert commands. We can then use those commands based on our requirements. Besides the assert commands available with the Nightwatch, we can also use the assert commands mentioned in the Node.js library here: **https://nodejs. org/api/assert.html**.

Nightwatch, a wrapper over Selenium, provides the assert library out of the box. So here, we do not have to use or add any other unit test framework that provides the capability to use assert commands for our script requirements. Besides its assert library, Nightwatch also provides us with a BDD-styled interface to perform assertions. These are based on the *Chai* expect assertion library. The link is here: **https://www.chaijs.com/api/bdd/**. *Chai* is a BDD/TDD assertion library for the browser and can be paired with any JavaScript testing framework.

In this chapter, we will see both **assert** commands and **expect** commands.

Assertions in Nightwatch

Assertions declare the outcome of the test. The output of any assert command is either true or false. We can understand the application's state under test based on these results. Let us look at the assert commands Nightwatch provides. The assert API of Nightwatch is here: **https://nightwatchjs.org/api/assert/**. The following table lists all the assert commands:

Serial number	Command	Description
1.	attributeContains	Usage: .assert.attributeContains(element, attribute, expected-value); This assert function verifies if for the given element's attributes, contains the expected value matches or not.
2.	attributeEquals	Usage: .assert.attributeEquals(element, attribute', expected-value); This assert function verifies if for the given element's attributes, exactly matches the expected value.
3.	attributeMatches	Usage: .assert.attributeMatches(element, attribute, regex expression); This assert function verifies the attribute for the given element, using a regular expression. So, if the attribute value matches the regular expression pattern, the function will pass.
4.	cssProperty	Usage: .assert.cssProperty(element, css property, expected-value); This assert function verifies if the css property of the given element is equal to the expected value.
5.	domPropertyContains	Usage: .assert.domPropertyContains(element, domProperty, expected-value); This assert function verifies if for the given element, the value associated with the given DOM property contains the expected value or not. For the list of DOM properties which could be given for the element are: https://developer.mozilla.org/en-US/docs/Web/API/element.
6.	domPropertyEquals	Usage: .assert.domPropertyEquals(element, domProperty, expected-value); This assert function verifies if for the given element, the value associated with the given DOM property is equal to the expected value or not. For the list of DOM properties which could be given for the element are: https://developer.mozilla.org/en-US/docs/Web/API/element

Serial number	Command	Description
7.	domPropertyMatches	Usage: .assert.domPropertyMatches(element, domProperty, expected-value); This assert function verifies if for the given element, the value associated with the given DOM property matches the regular expression pattern of the expected value or not. For the list of DOM properties which could be given for the element are: https://developer.mozilla.org/en-US/docs/Web/API/element
8.	elementsCount	Usage: .assert.elementsCount(element, count) This function verifies if the number of elements given are equal to the count. For example, we can verify how many div elements are present.
9.	elementPresent	Usage: .assert.elementPresent(element); This function verifies whether the element is present or not.
10.	hasClass	Usage: .assert.hasClass(element,className); This function verifies if the given element has the className provided in the assertion function or not.
11.	hasAttribute	Usage: .assert.hasAttribute(element,attribute); This function verifies if the given element has the attribute mentioned
12.	hasDescendants	Usage: .assert.hasDescendants('#main'); This function verifies if the given element has child elements or not.
13.	enabled	Usage: .assert.hasDescendants('#main'); This function verifies if the given element has child elements or not.
14.	selected	Usage: .assert.selected(element); This function verifies whether the element is selected or not, for example a radio button or a checkbox.
15.	textContains	Usage: .assert.textContains(element, 'text'); This function verifies whether the element contains a text or not.

Serial number	Command	Description
16.	textEquals	Usage: .assert.textEquals(element, 'text'); This function verifies whether the element has the exact text passed as argument or not.
17.	textMatches	Usage: .assert.textMatches(element, regex); This function verifies whether the element has the text which matches the given regular expression or not.
18.	titleContains	Usage: .assert.titleContains(Title); This function verifies whether the web page contains the title passed or not.
19.	titleEquals	Usage: .assert.titleContains(Title); This function verifies whether the web page contains the title passed or not.
20.	titleMatches	Usage: .assert.titleMatches(regex); This function verifies whether the web page title matches with the regular expression pattern passed.
21.	urlContains	Usage: .assert.titleMatches(regex); This function verifies whether the web page title matches with the regular expression pattern passed.
22.	urlEquals	Usage: .assert.urlEquals(url); This function verifies whether the URL of the web page is equal to the URL passed in the function.
23.	urlMatches	Usage: .assert.urlMatches(regex); This function verifies whether the URL of the webpage matches with the regular expression passed here.
24.	valueContains	Usage: .assert.valueContains(element, value); Form elements of web page, like a textbox have a field called as value. This function takes as input the web element and verifies whether the element value attribute data contains the argument, value passed here or not.

Serial number	Command	Description
25.	valueEquals	Usage: .assert.valueEquals(element, value); Form elements of web page, like a textbox have a field called as value. This function takes as input the web element and verifies whether the element value attribute data is equal to the argument, value passed here or not.
26.	visible	Usage: .assert.visible(element'); This function verifies if the passed element in the function is visible or not.

Table 8.1: List of assert commands

Thus, the above table shows the list of assertion commands Nightwatch has, their description, and their usage. Next, we will see how we can use these commands in the script.

Using assertions in script

In the previous section, we understood the usage of assertions. In this section, we will look at using the assertions in the script and see how they help us make a script into a test case. We will pick the login logout scenario from the BPB Practice web application for this. We will log in as an existing user and verify the action by asserting that the *Log Off* link is present. We will then log out and verify the action by asserting the absence of the *Log Off* link.

The steps for login and logout into the web application are as follows:

1. Open the application using the URL: **http://practice.bpbonline.com/**

2. Click on the **My Account** link, as shown in the following figure:

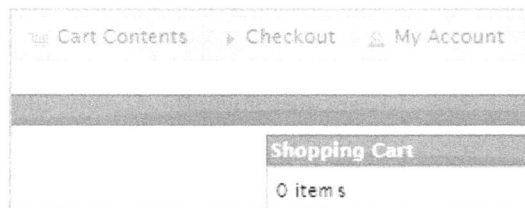

Figure 8.1: My Account link

3. On the next page (*Figure 8.2*), fill in the credentials for the username and password, which you may have used to create an account earlier. Further, click on the **Sign In** button.

Figure 8.2: Sign-in page

4. After logging in to the application, we will see the **Log Off** link. We will verify the presence of the object and use the assertion command, as shown in the following figure:

Figure 8.3: Log Off Link

5. We will then click on the **Log Off** link, followed by **Continue**, and return to the main page. Here, we will assert the absence of the **Log Off** link object, as shown in the following figure:

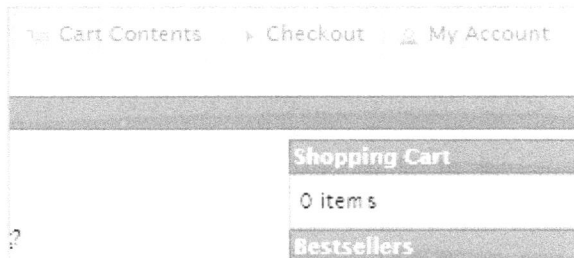

Figure 8.4: Main page, no Log Off link

The following script, which we can also call a test script since we are **asserting** our actions, is as follows:

```
1.    describe('Login Logout BPB', function() {
2.        before(browser => browser.navigateTo('http://practice.bpbonline.
    com/'));
3.        it('Register User BPB', function(browser) {
```

```
4.          browser
5.            .useXpath() //setting locator to be used as xpath for
    following commands
6.            .click('link text', 'My Account') //click on My Account link
7.            .setValue("//input[@name='email_address']", "bpb@bpb.com")//
    set email
8.            .setValue("//input[@name='password']", "bpb@123")//set  password
9.            .click("//button[@id='tdb5']")//click on Sign in button
10.           //add object presence assertion
11.           .assert.elementPresent("//*[contains(text(),'Log Off')]")
12.           .click('link text', 'Log Off')//click on Log Off link
13.           .click('link text', 'Continue')// Click on Continue link
14.           //add object absence assertion
15.           .assert.not.elementPresent("//*[contains(text(),'Log Off')]")
16.         });
17.
18.     after(browser => browser.end());
19.   });
```

We will see the following output in the IDE as we execute the script. Please note that we are using Visual Studio Code here:

```
Running Register User BPB:

√ Testing if element <//*[contains(text(),'Log Off')]> is present (26ms)
√ Testing if element <//*[contains(text(),'Log Off')]> is not present (39ms)

  PASSED. 2 assertions. (9.907s)
Wrote HTML report file to: D:\WORK\BPB PUBLICATIONS\NIGHTWATCH\TestProjectNWold\tests_output\nightwatch-html-report\index.html
```

Figure 8.5: Output of login logout with assertion

In the next section, let us look at what is expected and how we can use this verification form for the test script.

Understanding expect

expect is a **behavior-driven development** (**BDD**) style of assertion provided by Nightwatch, built over the assertion library Chai: **https://www.chaijs.com/api/bdd/**. Chai is a BDD/TDD assertion library for Node applications and can be used with any JavaScript-based testing framework, like Nightwatch. It provides significant flexibility over the default assert interface.

The benefit **expect** brings to the table is that it allows the chaining of commands. This means it allows us to add one command with others to create an assertion. The benefit is that it makes the assertion more human-readable. The following are called *chainable getters*, which we can use to create chains; they do not have testing capabilities but help us create a chain of command. They are as follows:

- to
- be
- been
- is
- that
- which
- and
- has
- have
- with
- at
- does
- of

Let us see an example of how we can use the chain getters to make an assertion command:

```
expect('foo').to.be.a('string');
```

The above expression says we expect **foo** to be a string. Another example is as follows:

```
expect([]).to.be.an('array').that.is.empty;
```

We expect **[ ]** to be an empty array. The above examples help us understand how to use the chain getters and create readable assertions.

expect also has other methods available, which perform assertions on the specified target of a given element. Let us have a look at them in *Table 8.2*:

Command	Explanation	Example
equal()	This will evaluate if the given value is equal to the expected.	browser.expect.element('#heading').text.to.equal('NightWatch');
contain()	This method finds if the given value is a part of the expected.	browser.expect.element('#heading').text.to.contain('Night');
match()	This method finds if based on a regular expression there is a match between the given and expected.	browser.expect.element('#heading').text.to.match('Night*');

Command	Explanation	Example
startWith()	This method finds, if the given value starts with expected.	browser.expect.element('#heading').text. to.startwith('Night*');
endWith()	This method finds if the given value ends with expected.	browser.expect.element('#heading').text. to.endWith('Night*');
not()	It negates any assertion given in the chain of command.	browser.expect.element('#heading').text. to.not.equal('NightWatch');
before()/ after()	These methods perform assertion, either before or after another assertion. This helps in adding a retry ability to the commands.	browser.expect.element('#heading').text. to.contain('NightWatch').before(1000); browser.expect.element('#heading').text. to.contain('NightWatch').after(1000);

Table 8.2: List of expect() methods for assertion

Thus, we have covered the **expect** command of Nightwatch. We will now see some example scripts that showcase its implementation.

Using expect in script

The first example we will see of **expect** is expecting an element to have text. For this, we will use the login logout scenario from the BPB Practice application. The steps are as follows:

1. Open the application using the following URL: **http://practice.bpbonline.com/**

2. Click on the **My Account** link, as shown in the following figure:

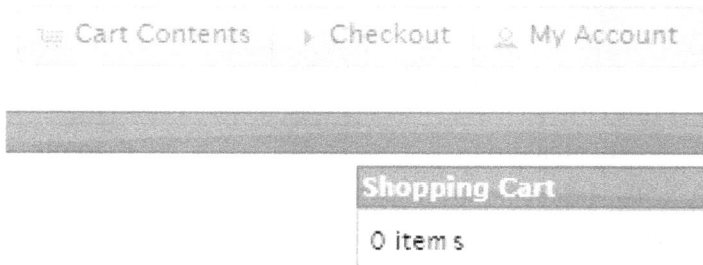

Figure 8.6: My Account link

3. On the next page, fill in the credentials for the username and password, using which you may have created an account earlier, and click on the **Sign In** button, as shown in the following figure:

Figure 8.7: Sign-in page

4. After logging into the application, we will see the **Log Off** link. We will verify the presence of the object and use the assertion command, as shown in the following figure:

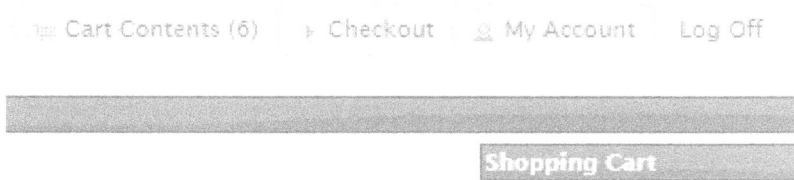

Figure 8.8: Log Off link

The following script showcases the use of *expect* to verify the Log Off link:

```
1.    describe('Login Logout BPB', function() {
2.        before(browser => browser.navigateTo('http://practice.bpbonline.
      com/'));
3.        it('Register User BPB', function(browser) {
4.            browser
5.              .useXpath() //setting locator to be used as xpath for
      following commands
6.              .click('link text', 'My Account') //click on My Account link
7.              .setValue("//input[@name='email_address']", "bpb@bpb.com")//
      set email
8.              .setValue("//input[@name='password']", "bpb@123")//set
      password
9.              .click("//button[@id='tdb5']")//click on Sign in button
10.             //add object presence assertion
```

```
11.              .expect.element("//a[@id='tdb4']").text.to.equal("Log Off")
12.          });
13.
14.      after(browser => browser.end());
15.    });
```

The output of the above script will be as follows:

```
Running Register User BPB:
────────────────────────────────────────────────────────────
 √ Expected element <//a[@id='tdb4']> text to equal: "Log Off" (37ms)

 ◈ PASSED. 1 assertions. (4.663s)
Wrote HTML report file to: D:\WORK\BPB PUBLICATIONS\NIGHTWATCH\TestProjectNWold\tests_output\nightwatch-html-report\index.html
```

Figure 8.9: Output of using expect

Let us take another example for **expect**, wherein we will use **expect** to verify whether the data we have typed in the username field, which sets the **value** attribute, is validated or not.

So, we type **bpb@bpb.com** into the email address and validate using **expect**, as shown in the following figure:

Returning Customer

I am a returning customer.

E-Mail Address: | bpb@bpb.com
Password: |

Password forgotten? Click here.

🖉 Sign In

Figure 8.10: Email field data

The script for the above is as follows:

```
1.    describe('Login Logout BPB', function() {
2.        before(browser => browser.navigateTo('http://practice.bpbonline.
      com/'));
3.        it('Register User BPB', function(browser) {
4.          browser
5.            .useXpath() //setting locator to be used as xpath for
      following commands
6.            .click('link text', 'My Account') //click on My Account Link
```

```
7.              .setValue("//input[@name='email_address']", "bpb@bpb.com")//
    set email
8.              .expect.element("//input[@name='email_address']").to.have.
    attribute('value').equals('bpb@bpb.com')
9.          });
10.         after(browser => browser.end());
11.     });
```

As we execute the script, we will see the following output:

```
√ Expected element <//input[@name='email_address']> to have attribute "value" equal to: "bpb@bpb.com" {28ms}

  PASSED. 1 assertions. (2.506s)
Wrote HTML report file to: D:\WORK\BPB PUBLICATIONS\NIGHTWATCH\TestProjectNWold\tests_output\nightwatch-html-report\index.html
```

Figure 8.11: Output of expecting value attribute data

Similarly, you can use **expect** for the scripts. To know more about it, check the link: **https://nightwatchjs.org/api/expect/**.

Conclusion

In this chapter, we learned about the importance of assertions for testing. We learned why we need to add assertions in the script, which helps them convert into test scripts. Adding assertions helps us validate the action the script is intended to perform. We saw the assert API of Nightwatch. The different methods that are available are as follows: We saw the usage of assertions for the login logout script. We then saw what was expected and how we can use it to add more readable validations to the script.

In the next chapter, we will learn how to work with the form elements of a web application.

Questions

1. What is the difference between textContains() and textEquals() method of assert?

2. Create an expect statement to match an element starting text.

Answers

1. The textEqual() method will match the exact value of the given with expected. Meanwhile, the textContains() assertion matches the substring of the given with expected.

2. browser.expect.element('#main').text.to.startWith('The');

Join our book's Discord space

Join the book's Discord Workspace for Latest updates, Offers, Tech happenings around the world, New Release and Sessions with the Authors:

https://discord.bpbonline.com

CHAPTER 9
Working with Form Elements

In the previous chapter, we learned how to use assertions in Nightwatch. With the help of assertion commands, we were able to convert our script into test scripts, which means we were able to validate the actions done on the web application. By validating the actions for expected, we can mark a test as pass or fail, which helps in the overall assessment of build quality. In this and the next few chapters, we will learn about different types of html elements and how using Nightwatch we can automate them. In this chapter, we will learn different Form elements available in a web application and how to automate those elements using Nightwatch commands. We will also see a few scripts based on what we learned about automation of the form elements.

Structure

In this chapter, we will discuss the following topics:
- Understanding HTML elements
- Understanding form elements
- Nightwatch commands to automate form elements

Objectives

By the end of this chapter, you will be able to understand html and Form elements. Further, you will learn about Nightwatch commands to automate form elements.

Understanding HTML elements

Hypertext Markup Language (HTML) is a standard markup language used to create web pages. It provides us with a set of rules for the layout and presentation of text, images, and objects on a web page. HTML tells the web browser how to display the content to the end user. A simple HTML document looks as follows where the section on the left side is a raw document, and on the right side is how it will be displayed on the browser:

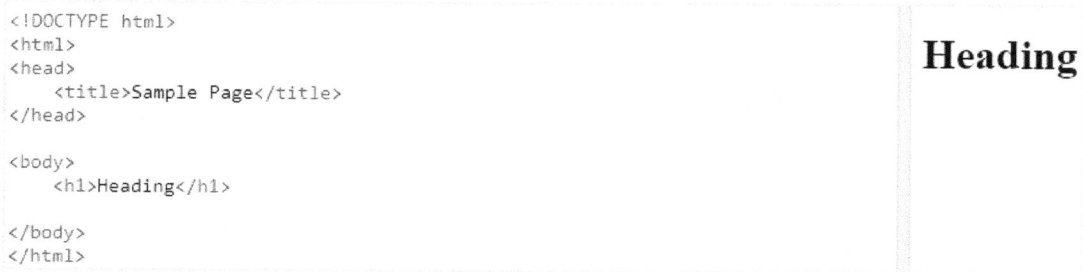

```
<!DOCTYPE html>
<html>
<head>
    <title>Sample Page</title>
</head>

<body>
    <h1>Heading</h1>

</body>
</html>
```

Heading

Figure 9.1: Image showing raw and rendered HTML document

An HTML document is made of HTML elements. It is represented by an opening tag and some content followed by a closing tag. HTML language has predefined tags. With the help of tags, a browser can interpret how to display and format the content provided for the end user. The complete list of html tags can be found here: **https://www.w3schools.com/tags/default.asp**

Any HTML element is created with the help of an HTML tag. The html element is represented as follows:

```
<tagname>Content goes here...</tagname>
```

Figure 9.2: HTML element representation

Let us try to see examples of HTML elements from a web page. For this, we will perform the following steps:

1. Open the URL on a Chrome browser: **https://practice.bpbonline.com/**

2. Click on the **My Account** link:

Cart Contents   Checkout   My Account

Figure 9.3: My Account link

3. When we click the **My Account** link, we see a form to fill out to log in to the application, as shown in the following figure:

Figure 9.4: Form for login to the application

4. We will now right-click on the email address text box and see in the context menu, a field **Inspect**. We will click on it:

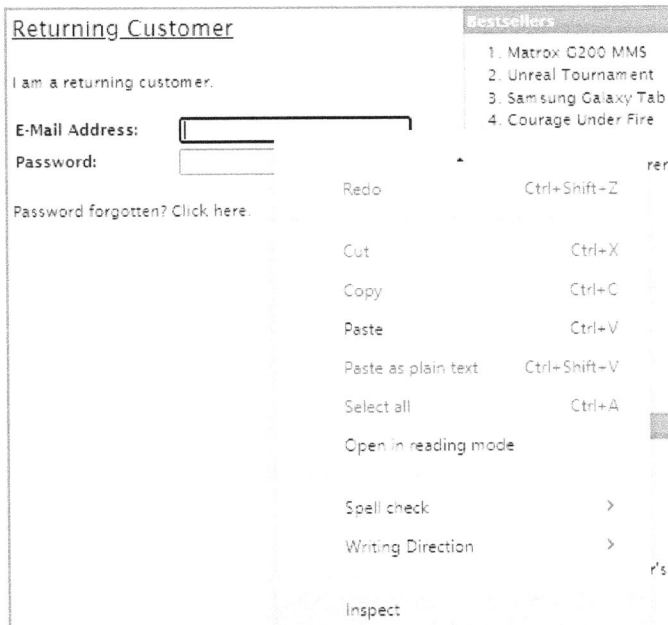

Figure 9.5: Inspect email address field

5. On clicking **Inspect**, we can see the HTML associated with this html element:

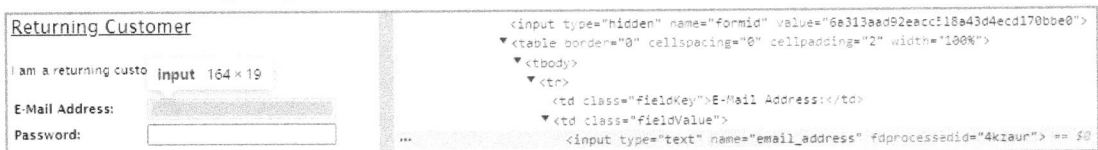

Figure 9.6: HTML associated with email address field

As seen in the preceding figure, the html element is represented with an input tag opening and closing. You can also do view page source to see the same.

```
<input type="text" name="email_address" />
```

Similar to above, we can explore other HTML elements in the page and find the html information associated with them. All elements will follow the pattern of a start tag, an end tag, and content in between them. Next, let us take a look at what the attributes of an html element.

HTML attributes

HTML attributes provide more details for an html element. Generally, the attributes associated with the html element depend on the type of html element. Let us take an example of a link we commonly see on a web page. To understand, we will take an example from the BPB website. The following steps will help us understand attribute:

1. Launch the application on a browser using the URL: **https://practice.bpbonline. com/**

2. Right-click on the **My Account** link we see on the page, as shown in the following figure:

Cart Contents　▸ Checkout　My Account

Figure 9.7: My Account link

3. You will find the following HTML associated with the element.

```
<a id="tdb3" href="https://practice.bpbonline.com/account.php"
class="ui-button ui-widget ui-state-default ui-button-text-icon-
primary ui-priority-secondary ui-corner-right" role="button" aria-
disabled="false"></a>
```

4. You can see that the link is represented using tag **<a>**, called the Anchor tag.

5. The attributes available are, **id**, **href**, **class**, and **role**.

Generally, one can find the **href** attribute specific to links or anchor html elements in an HTML page. The **href** informs which page to open when the link is clicked.

Similarly, we can find attributes associated with HTML elements in an html page of a web application. We will now discuss the types of html elements we come across in web applications and how to automate them. In the next section, we will discuss the Form element.

Understanding form elements

Form elements are HTML elements that are used to collect user input. The user input is generally sent to the server for processing. The HTML form element is a container element, which means it can contain other types of html elements. The following are the html elements that can be inside the form element: **<input>**, **<label>**, **<select>**, **<textarea>**, **<button>**, **<fieldset>**, **<legend>**, **<datalist>**, **<output>**, **<option>**, **<optgroup>**. Let us see them in detail.

- **<input>**

  An input element expects the user to share an input. It is the most commonly used element in forms. An input element has an important attribute called **type**. Based on the data associated with it, the information the end user has to fill in changes. An input element can have the following types:

  o **<input type="button">**
  o **<input type="checkbox">**
  o **<input type="color">**
  o **<input type="date">**
  o **<input type="datetime-local">**
  o **<input type="email">**
  o **<input type="file">**
  o **<input type="hidden">**
  o **<input type="image">**
  o **<input type="month">**
  o **<input type="number">**
  o **<input type="password">**
  o **<input type="radio">**
  o **<input type="range">**
  o **<input type="reset">**
  o **<input type="search">**
  o **<input type="submit">**
  o **<input type="tel">**
  o **<input type="text">**
  o **<input type="time">**
  o **<input type="url">**
  o **<input type="week">**

  An example input element is as follows:

```
<!DOCTYPE html>
<html>
<body>

<h2>Radio button</h2>

<form action="/action_page.php">
  <label for="fname">male</label>
  <input type="radio" id="fname" name="fname">
  <label for="lname">female</label>
  <input type="radio" id="lname" name="lname">
  <label for="thname">third gender</label>
  <input type="radio" id="thname" name="thname">
</form>

<p>Please select one</p>

</body>
</html>
```

Radio button

male ○ female ○ third gender ○

Please select one

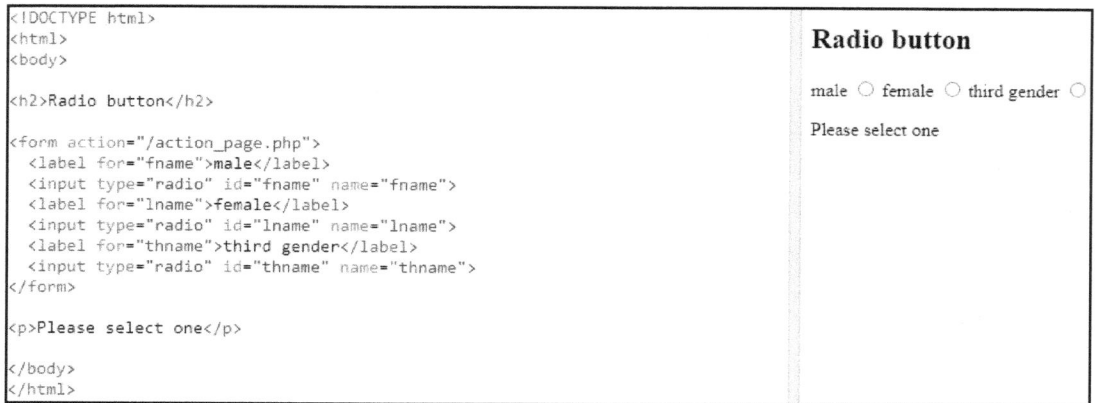

Figure 9.8: Input element example with HTML

- **<label>**

  The label tag helps define the label for other elements. It is also used by screen readers to focus on the input element. In *Figure 9.8,* we can see the use of a **label** tag with the input field for the web page. The labels are used with another element to describe and guide users about it.

- **<select>**

  The select tag represents a drop-down for an html page. It is also a container element and contains another html tag called an option. We will talk more about the drop-down in the next chapter. A form element can contain a select element. For example, we are fetching user information and want to fetch the country the user belongs to.

  Let us see an example of select within a form:

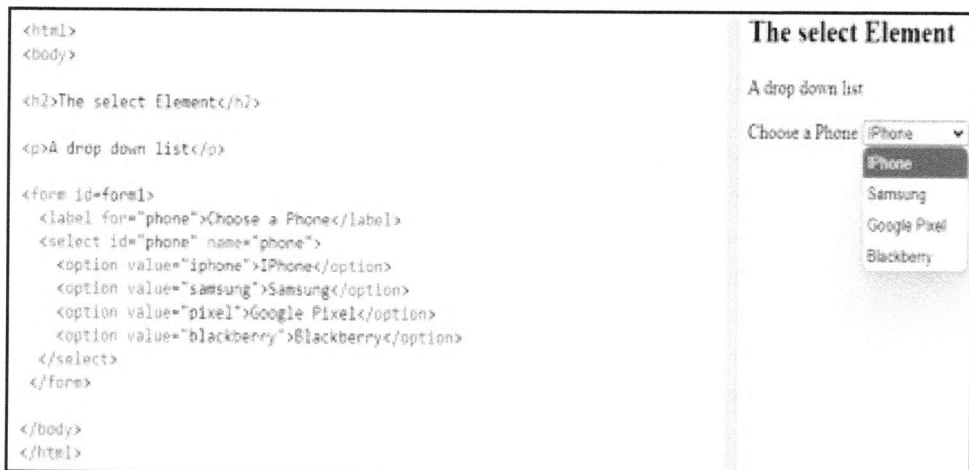

```
<html>
<body>

<h2>The select Element</h2>

<p>A drop down list</p>

<form id=form1>
  <label for="phone">Choose a Phone</label>
  <select id="phone" name="phone">
    <option value="iphone">IPhone</option>
    <option value="samsung">Samsung</option>
    <option value="pixel">Google Pixel</option>
    <option value="blackberry">Blackberry</option>
  </select>
</form>

</body>
</html>
```

The select Element

A drop down list

Choose a Phone IPhone ▼

IPhone
Samsung
Google Pixel
Blackberry

Figure 9.9: Drop-down element in form

- **<textarea>**

  The **textarea** HTML tag helps represent an HTML element that allows multiline text input. We use attributes, rows, and columns to define the size of the **textarea** field.

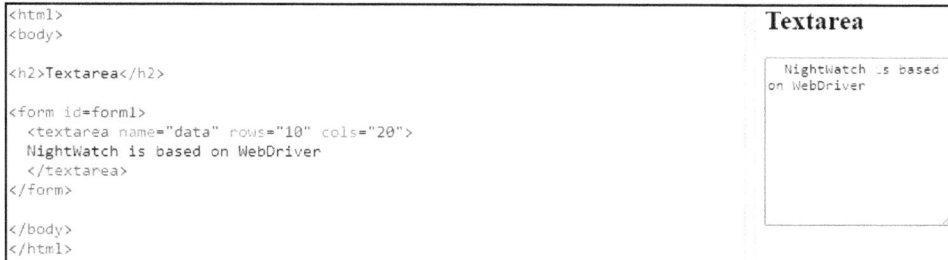

```
<html>
<body>

<h2>Textarea</h2>

<form id=form1>
  <textarea name="data" rows="10" cols="20">
  NightWatch is based on WebDriver
  </textarea>
</form>

</body>
</html>
```

Textarea

```
NightWatch is based
on WebDriver
```

Figure 9.10: An example of the text area tag element

- **<button>**

  The **button** tag helps create a clickable button element.

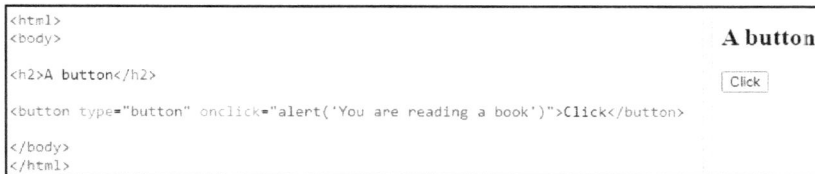

```
<html>
<body>

<h2>A button</h2>

<button type="button" onclick="alert('You are reading a book')">Click</button>

</body>
</html>
```

A button

```
Click
```

Figure 9.11: An example of the button element

- **<fieldset>**

  The **fieldset** tag helps group similar elements for a form. It draws a tag around related elements. We will see the **fieldset** and legend together in the following example.

- **<legend>**

  The **legend** tag helps give a caption **fieldset**. We generally use legend with **fieldset**. In the following figure, you will see how **fieldset** and legend define a section for customer information:

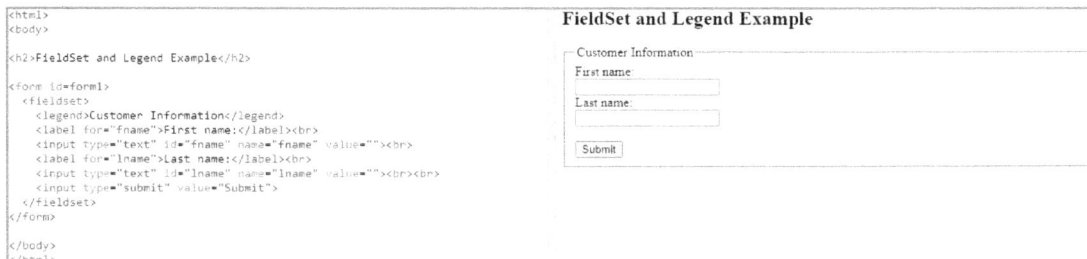

```
<html>
<body>

<h2>FieldSet and Legend Example</h2>

<form id=form1>
  <fieldset>
    <legend>Customer Information</legend>
    <label for="fname">First name:</label><br>
    <input type="text" id="fname" name="fname" value=""><br>
    <label for="lname">Last name:</label><br>
    <input type="text" id="lname" name="lname" value=""><br><br>
    <input type="submit" value="Submit">
  </fieldset>
</form>

</body>
</html>
```

FieldSet and Legend Example

```
┌─ Customer Information ──────────
  First name:
  [              ]
  Last name:
  [              ]

  [ Submit ]
```

Figure 9.12: An example of the fieldset with legend

- **<datalist>**

  The **datalist** tag helps define predefined data points for an input element. The end user will only be able to choose from there. Here, we need to ensure that the **list** attribute for the input tag is the same as the id attribute of the **datalist** tag. Let us see an example:

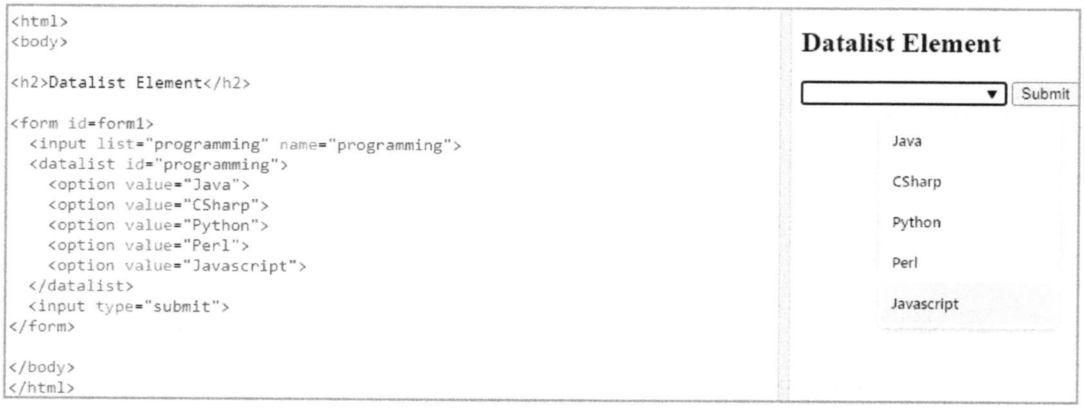

```html
<html>
<body>

<h2>Datalist Element</h2>

<form id=form1>
  <input list="programming" name="programming">
  <datalist id="programming">
    <option value="Java">
    <option value="CSharp">
    <option value="Python">
    <option value="Perl">
    <option value="Javascript">
  </datalist>
  <input type="submit">
</form>

</body>
</html>
```

Datalist Element

Java

CSharp

Python

Perl

Javascript

Figure 9.13: An example of the datalist element

- **<output>**

  The output element displays the result of a calculation. Let us see with an example where we add data from two numbers and a range element:

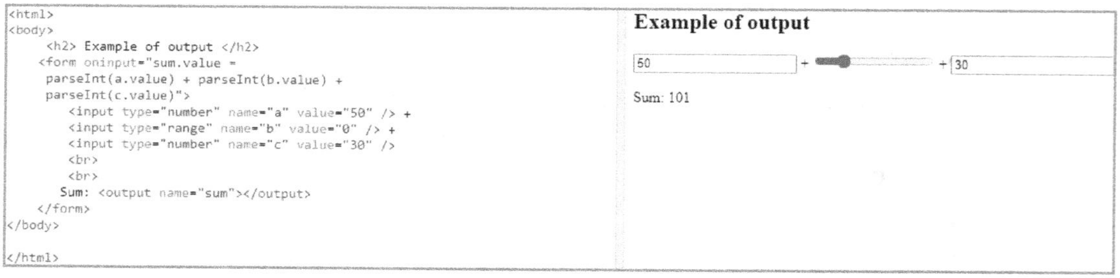

```html
<html>
<body>
    <h2> Example of output </h2>
    <form oninput="sum.value =
    parseInt(a.value) + parseInt(b.value) +
    parseInt(c.value)">
        <input type="number" name="a" value="50" /> +
        <input type="range" name="b" value="0" /> +
        <input type="number" name="c" value="30" />
        <br>
        <br>
    Sum: <output name="sum"></output>
    </form>
</body>

</html>
```

Example of output

50   +   + 30

Sum: 101

Figure 9.14: An example of output element

- **<option>**

  The **option** tag defines the option in the drop-down list created using the **<select>** tag. This tag can be used inside **select**, **datalist**, or **optgroup**. We have seen the use of option with select and **datalist**. With the next tag, **optgroup** we will see its usage with it.

- **<optgroup>**

  The **optgroup** tag is used to group related options in the **select** element. Let us see its usage with example.

```
<html>
<body>
    <h2>Example for optgroup</h2>
    <select>
        <optgroup label="Programming Languages">
            <option value="Java">java</option>
            <option value="C++">C++</option>
            <option value="dotnet">VB.net</option>
        </optgroup>
        <optgroup label="Scripting Language">
            <option value="Python">Python</option>
            <option value="Perl">Perl</option>
            <option value="Javascript">Javascript</option>
        </optgroup>
    </select>
</body>
</html>
```

Example for optgroup

java ▼

Programming Languages
java
C++
VB.net
Scripting Language
Python
Perl
Javascript

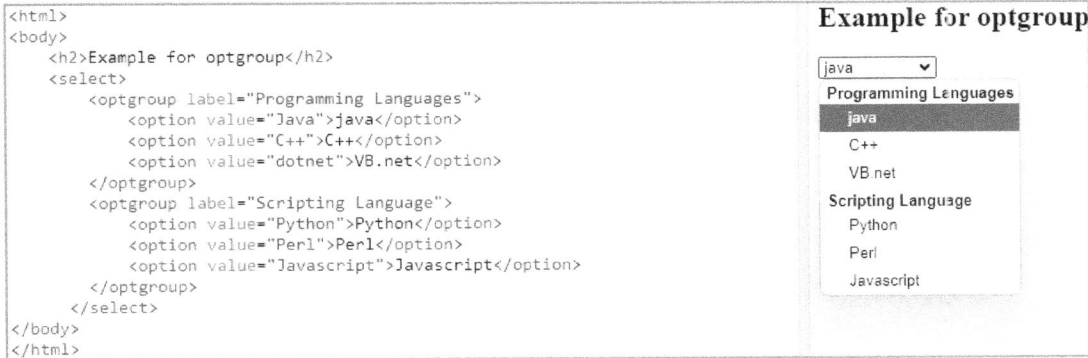

Figure 9.15: An example for optgroup

With this, we have discussed all the types of tags that can be a part of a *Form* element. The most commonly used tag in form is the input tag. We saw that an input tag can be of different kinds depending on the **type** attribute associated with the input element. Based on the type, the input tag element is displayed and performs its functions. For example, when we have an input tag element of **type** text, it will be displayed as a textbox and will function as a textbox that accepts user input. Similarly, if the input has **type** radio, we will see it as a radio button, which the user clicks to choose.

We will now see different commands that can be used to automate form elements with Nightwatch.

Nightwatch commands to automate form elements

In *Chapter 6, Interacting with Web Elements*, we explored the commands available with Nightwatch that we can use to interact with the Web Elements. We will take an example of a register user scenario to understand the form element, the types of elements in the form element, and how to use different commands to automate them. Let us first see the steps to register a user in the application, and then write down the script that will automate the user actions:

1. Launch the application using the URL, **https://practice.bpbonline.com/**. Click on the **My Account** link, as shown in the following figure:

Cart Contents ▸ Checkout ○ My Account

Figure 9.16: My Account link

2. To register as a new user, click on the continue button under **New Customer** section, as shown in the following figure:

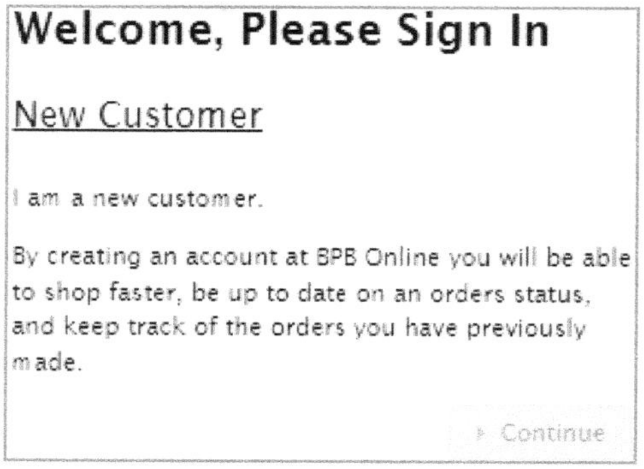

Figure 9.17: *Click on Continue to go to register user page*

3. Once you are on the new user registration page, you will find various fields. The fields that have a red asterisk are mandatory to be filled.

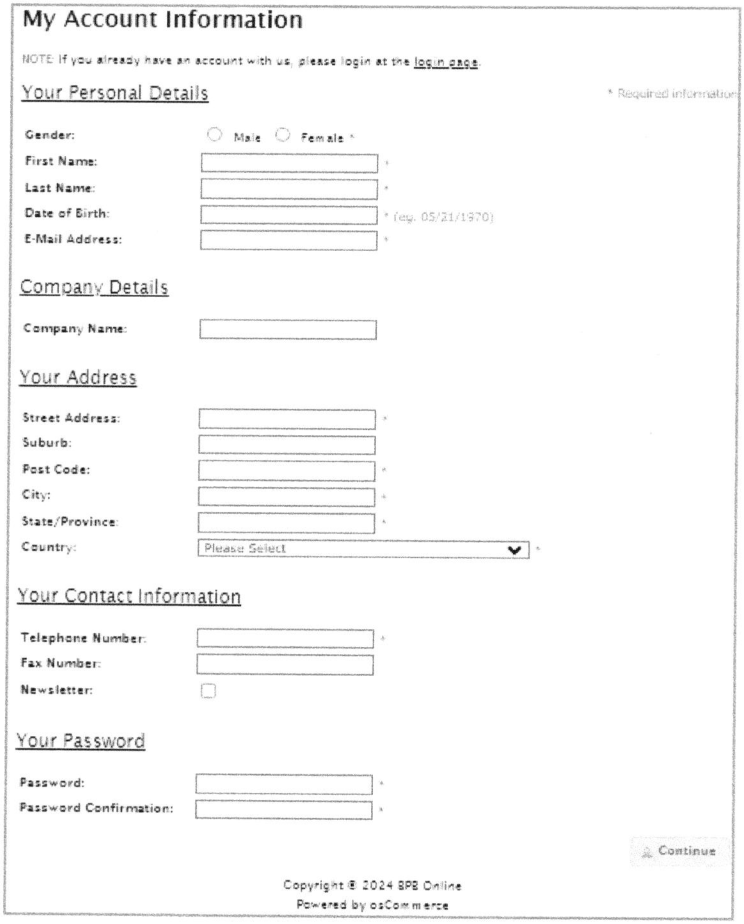

Figure 9.18: *Registration form*

4. Let us see the HTML content associated with this section to understand the different HTML elements shown here:

```
1.   <form name="create_account" action="https://practice.bpbonline.
     com/create_account.php?osCsid=8b4b578d6e3394dd71193932990520b7"
     method="post" onsubmit="return check_form(create_
     account);"><input type="hidden" name="formid"
     value="056150ec928bafe3017f7e61ae3ec7ea" /><input type="hidden"
     name="action" value="process" />
2.   <div class="contentContainer">
3.     <div>
4.       <span class="inputRequirement" style="float: right;">*
     Required information</span>
5.         <h2>Your Personal Details</h2>
6.     </div>
7.
8.   <div class="contentText">
9.       <table border="0" cellspacing="2" cellpadding="2"
     width="100%">
10.
11.
12.         <tr>
13.           <td class="fieldKey">Gender:</td>
14.           <td class="fieldValue"><input type="radio" name="gender"
     value="m" />  Male  <input type="radio"
     name="gender" value="f" />  Female <span
     class="inputRequirement">*</span></td>
15.         </tr>
16.
17.
18.         <tr>
19.           <td class="fieldKey">First Name:</td>
20.           <td class="fieldValue"><input type="text" name="firstname"
     /> <span class="inputRequirement">*</span></td>
21.         </tr>
22.         <tr>
23.           <td class="fieldKey">Last Name:</td>
24.           <td class="fieldValue"><input type="text" name="lastname"
     /> <span class="inputRequirement">*</span></td>
25.         </tr>
```

```
26.
27.
28.        <tr>
29.          <td class="fieldKey">Date of Birth:</td>
30.          <td class="fieldValue"><input type="text" name="dob"
      id="dob" /> <span class="inputRequirement">* (eg.
      05/21/1970)</span><script type="text/javascript">$('#dob').
      datepicker({dateFormat: 'mm/dd/yy', changeMonth: true,
      changeYear: true, yearRange: '-100:+0'});</script></td>
31.        </tr>
32.
33.
34.        <tr>
35.          <td class="fieldKey">E-Mail Address:</td>
36.          <td class="fieldValue"><input type="text" name="email_
      address" /> <span class="inputRequirement">*</span></td>
37.        </tr>
38.      </table>
39.    </div>
40.
41.
42.    <h2>Company Details</h2>
43.
44.    <div class="contentText">
45.      <table border="0" cellspacing="2" cellpadding="2"
      width="100%">
46.        <tr>
47.          <td class="fieldKey">Company Name:</td>
48.          <td class="fieldValue"><input type="text" name="company"
      /> </td>
49.        </tr>
50.      </table>
51.    </div>
52.
53.
54.    <h2>Your Address</h2>
55.
56.    <div class="contentText">
```

```
57.        <table border="0" cellspacing="2" cellpadding="2"
    width="100%">
58.          <tr>
59.            <td class="fieldKey">Street Address:</td>
60.            <td class="fieldValue"><input type="text" name="street_
    address" /> <span class="inputRequirement">*</span></td>
61.          </tr>
62.
63.
64.          <tr>
65.            <td class="fieldKey">Suburb:</td>
66.            <td class="fieldValue"><input type="text" name="suburb"
    /> </td>
67.          </tr>
68.
69.
70.          <tr>
71.            <td class="fieldKey">Post Code:</td>
72.            <td class="fieldValue"><input type="text" name='postcode"
    /> <span class="inputRequirement">*</span></td>
73.          </tr>
74.          <tr>
75.            <td class="fieldKey">City:</td>
76.            <td class="fieldValue"><input type="text" name="city"
    /> <span class="inputRequirement">*</span></td>
77.          </tr>
78.
79.
80.          <tr>
81.            <td class="fieldKey">State/Province:</td>
82.            <td class="fieldValue">
83.  <input type="text" name="state" /> <span
    class="inputRequirement">*</span>            </td>
84.          </tr>
85.
86.
87.          <tr>
88.            <td class="fieldKey">Country:</td>
```

```
89.            <td class="fieldValue"><select name="country"><option
      value="" selected="selected">Please Select</option><option
      value="1">Afghanistan</option>..
       <option value="239">Zimbabwe</option>
      </select> <span class="inputRequirement">*</span></td>
90.          </tr>
91.        </table>
92.      </div>
93.
94.      <h2>Your Contact Information</h2>
95.
96.      <div class="contentText">
97.        <table border="0" cellspacing="2" cellpadding="2"
      width="100%">
98.          <tr>
99.            <td class="fieldKey">Telephone Number:</td>
100.           <td class="fieldValue"><input type="text" name="telephone"
      /> <span class="inputRequirement">*</span></td>
101.         </tr>
102.         <tr>
103.           <td class="fieldKey">Fax Number:</td>
104.           <td class="fieldValue"><input type="text" name="fax"
      /> </td>
105.         </tr>
106.         <tr>
107.           <td class="fieldKey">Newsletter:</td>
108.           <td class="fieldValue"><input type="checkbox"
      name="newsletter" value="1" /> </td>
109.         </tr>
110.       </table>
111.     </div>
112.
113.     <h2>Your Password</h2>
114.
115.     <div class="contentText">
116.       <table border="0" cellspacing="2" cellpadding="2"
      width="100%">
117.         <tr>
118.           <td class="fieldKey">Password:</td>
```

```
119.              <td class="fieldValue"><input type="password"
       name="password" maxlength="40" /> <span
       class="inputRequirement">*</span></td>
120.          </tr>
121.          <tr>
122.            <td class="fieldKey">Password Confirmation:</td>
123.            <td class="fieldValue"><input type="password"
       name="confirmation" maxlength="40" /> <span
       class="inputRequirement">*</span></td>
124.          </tr>
125.        </table>
126.      </div>
127.
128.      <div class="buttonSet">
129.        <span class="buttonAction"><span class="tdbLink"><button
       id="tdb4" type="submit">Continue</button></span><script
       type="text/javascript">$("#tdb4").button({icons:{primary:"ui-
       icon-person"}}).addClass("ui-priority-primary").parent().
       removeClass("tdbLink");</script></span>
130.      </div>
131.    </div>
132.
133.  </form>
```

The content of HTML shows that we have a form element, which contains various elements that we see on the page. We have the radio button, checkbox, textboxes, drop down, password text box, button etc., displayed on the page. Not, let us look at the script where we will fill in all the mandatory fields and proceed with user registration.

1. Fill in all the details and click on the **Continue** button, as shown in the following figure:

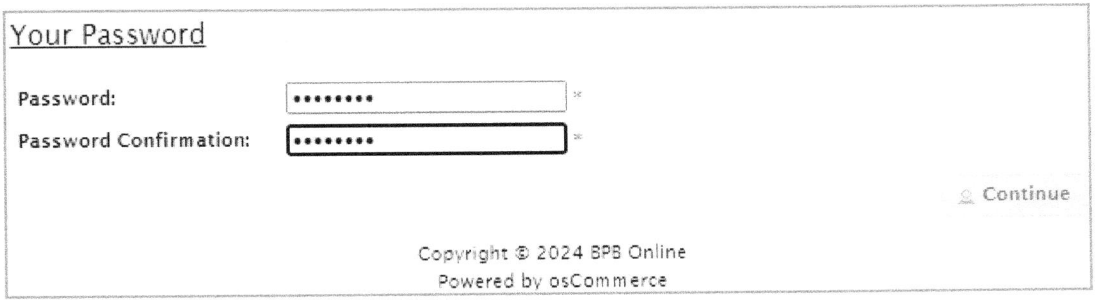

Figure 9.19: Continue button for user registration

2. Once the account is created, you will see the message about it. Clicking on the **Continue** button will allow you to explore the application as a registered user. This is shown in the following figure:

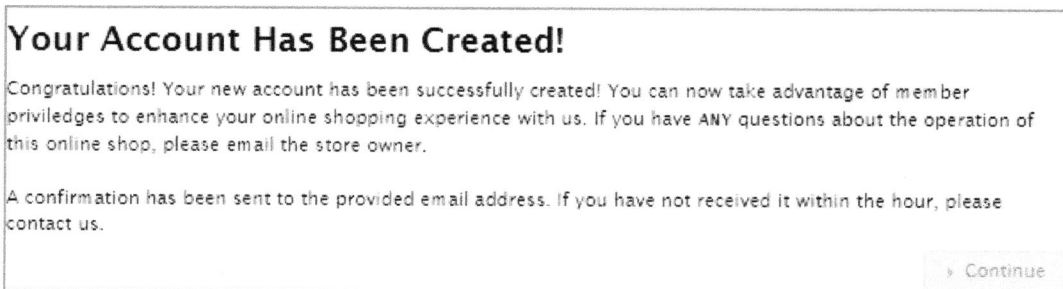

Your Account Has Been Created!

Congratulations! Your new account has been successfully created! You can now take advantage of member priviledges to enhance your online shopping experience with us. If you have ANY questions about the operation of this online shop, please email the store owner.

A confirmation has been sent to the provided email address. If you have not received it within the hour, please contact us.

> Continue

Figure 9.20: Account creation confirmation

As we write the script to automate the steps to register a user, we need to be careful at the time of execution. We need to understand that every time the script runs, it will register a new user. For this, it will need a new email address. If we do not change the email address with every script execution, the functional flow will fail. For this, we will use a random number generator and pass it with the email address string. Let us now see the script.

```
1.    describe('Register User BPB', function() {
2.        before(browser => browser.navigateTo('http://practice.
       bpbonline.com/'));
3.        it('Register User BPB', function(browser) {
4.          let email="test"+Math.random()+"@test.com"
5.          browser
6.            .useXpath() //setting locator to be used as xpath for
       following commands
7.            .click('link text', 'My Account') //click on My Account
       link
8.            .click("//a[@id='tdb4']")//click on Continue button
9.            //add object presence assertion
10.           .assert.elementPresent("//input[@name='firstname']")
11.           .click("//input[@name='gender'][@value='f']")
12.           .sendKeys("//input[@name='firstname']", "BPB")
13.           .sendKeys("//input[@name='lastname']", "Online")
14.           .sendKeys("//input[@name='dob']", "01/01/2000")
15.           .sendKeys("//input[@name='email_address']",email)
16.           .sendKeys("//input[@name='street_address']", "Hauz
       Khas")
17.           .sendKeys("//input[@name='postcode']", "12345")
```

```
18.            .sendKeys("//input[@name='city']", "New Delhi")
19.            .sendKeys("//input[@name='state']", "New Delhi")
20.            .setValue("//select[@name='country']","India")
21.            .sendKeys("//input[@name='telephone']", "1234567890")
22.            .sendKeys("//input[@name='password']", "test@123")
23.            .sendKeys("//input[@name='confirmation']", "test@123")
24.            //click to continue to register
25.            .click("//a[@id='tdb5']")
26.            //Click on Continue button for account
27.            .click("//button[@id='tdb4']")//click on Continue button
28.            //click to log off
29.            .click('link text', 'Log Off')//click on Log Off link
30.            .click('link text', 'Continue')// Click on Continue link
31.            //add object absence assertion
32.            .assert.not.elementPresent("//*[contains(text(),'Log
      Off')]")
33.          });
34.
35.        after(browser => browser.end());
36.      });
37.
```

When we execute the above script, we will find the action being done on various form elements on the register user page, and the user will get registered to the application. Also, note that the script has assertion mentioned to validate the action being done.

Thus, in this chapter, we explored various form elements that we can find in an html document and how we can use Nightwatch to automate actions on them.

Conclusion

In this chapter, we learned about html elements. We learned how they are represented using tags. We also saw that an html element can have various attributes. We then explored form elements and saw various types of elements that can be within the form element. We further explored different kinds of input elements and how, based on type, they change. We finally saw the automation of the form element with Nightwatch commands.

In the next chapter, we will learn how to work with other types of web elements.

Questions

1. What are form elements?

2. How to create a radio button in html?

Answers

1. Form elements are html elements that help create a form to fetch user input and pass it to the server.

2. A radio button is an input element defined with the value - radio for the type attribute.

Join our book's Discord space

Join the book's Discord Workspace for Latest updates, Offers, Tech happenings around the world, New Release and Sessions with the Authors:

https://discord.bpbonline.com

CHAPTER 10

Working with Tables, Drop-downs, Frames and Alerts

In the previous chapter, we learned about the Form element which is one of the common html elements found in a web page. We also learned about the various elements the Form element can contain and how they can be used. In this chapter, we will see a few more html elements and how we can automate them using Nightwatch. The elements which we will see in this chapter are—Table, drop down, frames and alerts. We will understand these html elements. We will see some scenarios where we can encounter these web elements. Finally, we will understand how to automate these elements using Nightwatch.

Structure

In this chapter, we will discuss the following topics:

- Understanding tables and automating them
- Understanding drop-down elements and automating them
- Understanding iFrames and automating them
- Understanding alerts and automating them

Objectives

By the end of this chapter, you will be able to understand tables, drop-down, frames, and alert web elements. You will also be able to understand different scenarios where we can encounter these elements. Finally, you will understand how to automate those scenarios using Nightwatch.

Understanding tables and automating them

HTML tables are container html elements, i.e., they contain other HTML elements. An HTML table contains rows and columns and defines a table cell. It is the cell that contains information like text or any other HTML element, which is shown to the end user for interaction. Let us define a simple HTML table and understand it more:

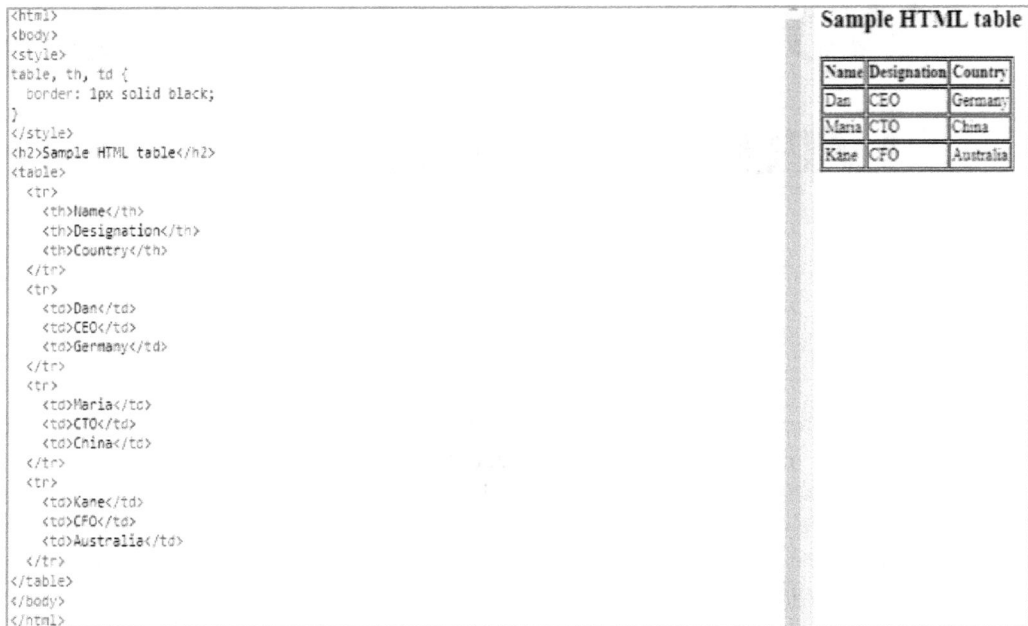

```
<html>
<body>
<style>
table, th, td {
  border: 1px solid black;
}
</style>
<h2>Sample HTML table</h2>
<table>
  <tr>
    <th>Name</th>
    <th>Designation</th>
    <th>Country</th>
  </tr>
  <tr>
    <td>Dan</td>
    <td>CEO</td>
    <td>Germany</td>
  </tr>
  <tr>
    <td>Maria</td>
    <td>CTO</td>
    <td>China</td>
  </tr>
  <tr>
    <td>Kane</td>
    <td>CFO</td>
    <td>Australia</td>
  </tr>
</table>
</body>
</html>
```

Sample HTML table

Name	Designation	Country
Dan	CEO	Germany
Maria	CTO	China
Kane	CFO	Australia

Figure 10.1: Sample HTML table

As we can see from *Figure 10.1*, the HTML table is defined using the **<table>** tag. This tag will further contain other HTML tags, which help define other elements of the table. Let us see the tags that become a part of the main table tag, which helps define it:

- **<tr>**

    The **<tr>** tag represents the table row. A **<tr>** tag will contain the table data tag, which helps define columns. The table will contain as many rows as the number of **<tr>** tags. For example, in *Figure 10.1*, we can see there are three **<tr>** tags that represent three rows.

- **<td>**

    The **<td>** tag represents table data. It is a child tag under the table row **<tr>** tag. It helps define columns within a table. For example, we can see in *Figure 10.1*, there are three **<td>** tags inside each **<tr>** tag, which showcases three columns in the table.

- **<th>**

    The **<th>** tag means table heading. It helps provide a heading for the table column and is generally used there. For example, let us see a table with a table header used.

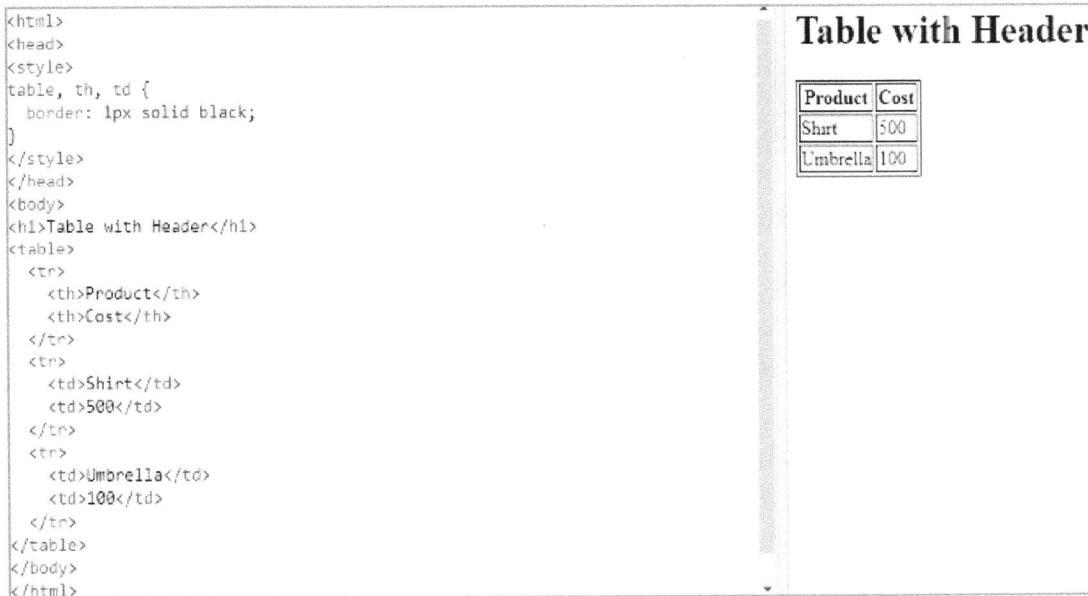

```
<html>
<head>
<style>
table, th, td {
  border: 1px solid black;
}
</style>
</head>
<body>
<h1>Table with Header</h1>
<table>
   <tr>
     <th>Product</th>
     <th>Cost</th>
   </tr>
   <tr>
     <td>Shirt</td>
     <td>500</td>
   </tr>
   <tr>
     <td>Umbrella</td>
     <td>100</td>
   </tr>
</table>
</body>
</html>
```

Table with Header

Product	Cost
Shirt	500
Umbrella	100

Figure 10.2: Table with header tag

There are other tags also that an html table can contain. You can find more information from this link **https://www.w3schools.com/html/html_tables.asp**. What we have seen above are the basic and crucial tags required to define a table. A table cell that gets defined with a **<tr>** and **<td>** tag can contain any html element, i.e., it can contain text, a button, a link, an image, or an input field. A web application uses a web table to represent data in a tabular format, and the table cell contains information for the end user to interact with. We generally automate a web table by iterating through its rows and columns, which we should pick dynamically from the application. Further, we can interact with the cell of interest to fetch the text present there or interact with an html element inside the table cell. Let us now understand how to automate a web table with the help of an example from the web application. The steps are as follows:

1. Launch the application on the browser using the URL: **https://practice.bpbonline. com/**:

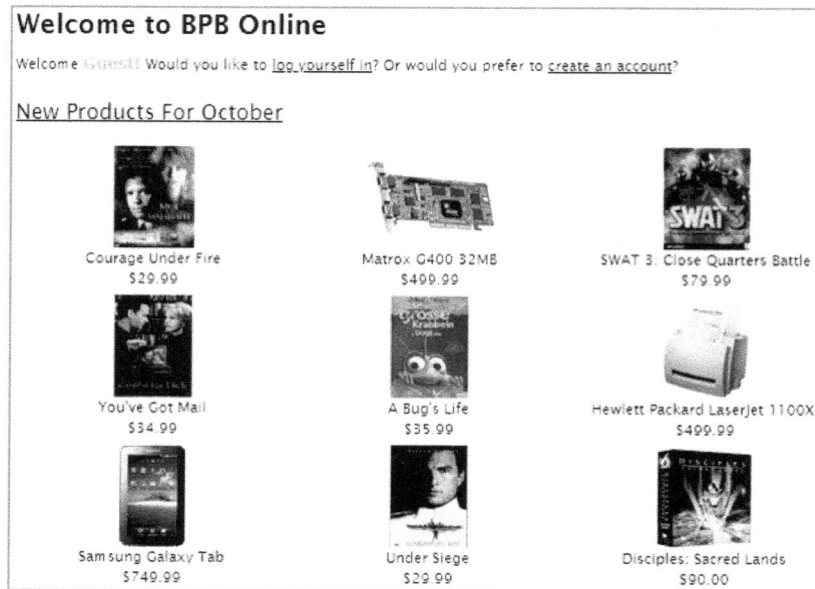

Figure 10.3: The home page of the application

2. The page shown in *Figure 10.3* is effectively a web table. As we do inspect elements, we can see the web table associated here as follows:

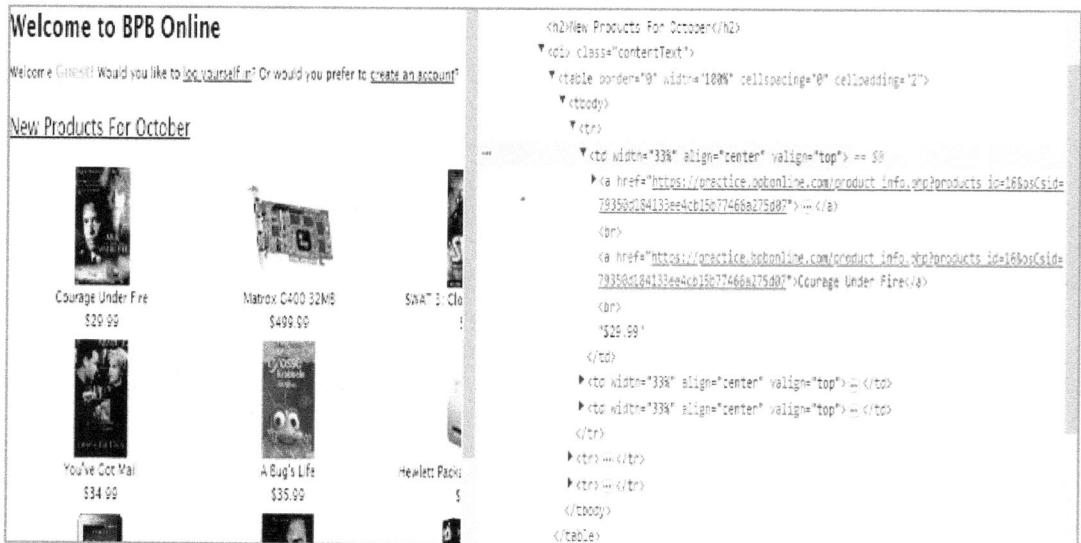

Figure 10.4: Web table

3. As shown in *Figure 10.4*, the web table displays products. It has three rows, where each row has three columns. Inside each cell, there are three elements: two anchor tags and a text displaying the price.

4. We will now write a script that will traverse the table and print in the output the names of the products and the prices associated with them.

Let us have a look at the following script for it:

```
1. describe('Traverse Product Table', function () {
2.   before(browser => browser.navigateTo('http://practice.
bpbonline.com/'));
3.
4.   it('Traverse Product Table', function (browser) {
5.     browser
6.       .useXpath() // Setting locator to be used as xpath for
following commands
7.       .assert.elementPresent("//*[contains(text(),'My
Account')]")
8.       .elements("css selector", "tr", function (fetchRows) {
9.         // fetchRows.value is an array of element objects
10.          const numberOfRows = fetchRows.value.length;
11.          console.log("Table rows: " + numberOfRows);
12.
13.          // Fetch table columns after getting rows
14.          browser.elements("css selector", "tr:nth-
child(1) td", function (fetchCols) {
15.            const numberOfCols = fetchCols.value.length;
16.            console.log("Table columns: " +
numberOfCols);
17.
18.            // Traverse table cells
19.            for (let i = 1; i <= numberOfRows; i++) {
20.              for (let j = 1; j <= numberOfCols; j++) {
21.                // Using XPath with correct format in
getText
22.                browser.getText(`//table/tbody/tr[${i}]/
td[${j}]`, function (result) {
23.                  console.log(`Row: ${i}, Column: ${j},
Value: ${result.value}`);
24.                });
25.              }
26.              break; // To print only first row
27.            }
28.          });
```

```
29.                });
30.            });
31.
32.        after(browser => browser.end());
33.    });
```

As the above code executes, we will find that all rows of the table are fetched, and the count of them, which is 3, is printed. Then, all **<td>** tags are fetched and their total count, i.e., 9, is printed. Finally, we see the output of one entire row. We break and exit the code. The output is as follows:

```
Running Traverse Product Table:

√ Testing if element <//*[contains(text(),'My Account')]> is present (37ms)
Table rows: 3
Table columns: 3
Row: 1, Column: 1, Value: Courage Under Fire
$29.99
Row: 1, Column: 2, Value: Matrox G400 32MB
$499.99
Row: 1, Column: 3, Value: SWAT 3: Close Quarters Battle
$79.99

✓ PASSED. 1 assertions. (465ms)
```

Figure 10.5: Output of table traverse program

Next, we will see how to handle and automate drop-down elements.

Understanding drop-down elements and automating them

The drop-down elements are common html elements that we see on a web application. They are created using the **<select>** tag. A **<select>** tag is a container tag, which means it contains other child tags. The **<select>** tag contains **<option>** tag. Every input associated with **<option>** is displayed in the drop-down list, which we see on the web page. For example, we can see a drop-down showing countries on the registration page of the application. The following steps will be needed to reach the register user page to access the drop-down:

1. Launch the application on the browser using the URL: **https://practice.bpbonline. com/**

2. Click on the **My Account** link, as shown in the following figure:

Cart Contents   Checkout   My Account

Figure 10.6: My Account link

3. Click on the **Continue** button for new user registration, as shown in the following figure:

Welcome, Please Sign In

New Customer

I am a new customer.

By creating an account at BPB Online you will be able to shop faster, be up to date on an orders status, and keep track of the orders you have previously made.

▹ Continue

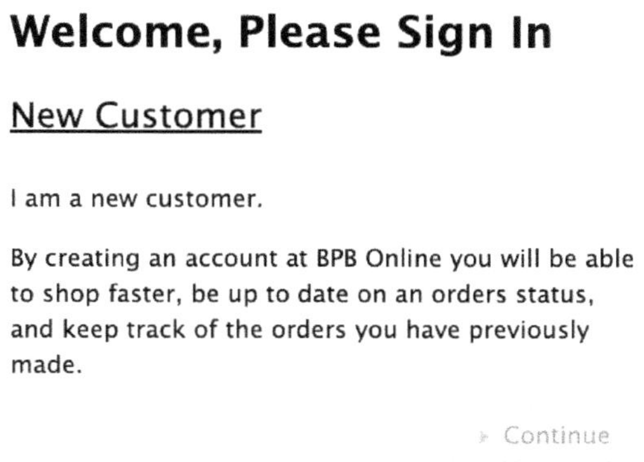

Figure 10.7: Continue button

4. We can now scroll down the page and reach the **Your Address** section. Here, we can see the country drop-down, as shown in the following figure:

Your Address

Street Address:		*
Suburb:		
Post Code:		*
City:		*
State/Province:		*
Country:	✓ Please Select	

Afghanistan

Your Contact Inforn Albania

Algeria

Telephone Number: American Samoa

Andorra

Fax Number: Angola

Newsletter: Anguilla

Antarctica

Your Password Antigua and Barbuda

Argentina

Password: Armenia

Aruba

Password Confirmation:

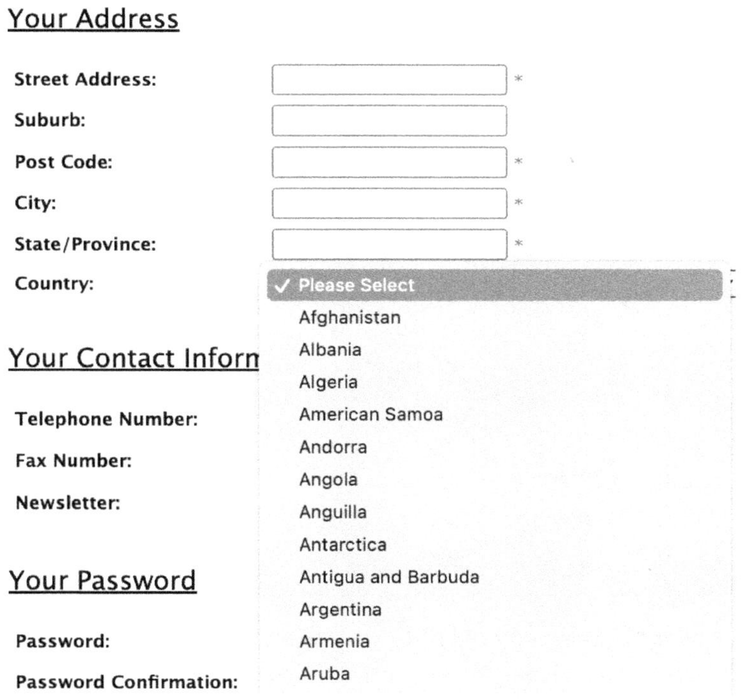

Figure 10.8: Country drop-down list

We can now inspect the element to see the html content associated with it, as shown in the following figure:

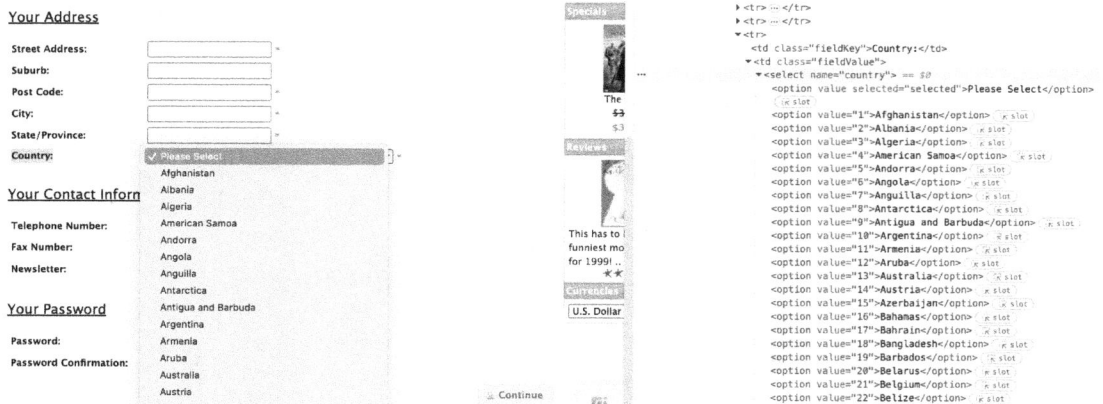

Figure 10.9: Drop-down list of countries with the select tag details

There are various scenarios we can perform on the drop-down list. For example, we can:

- Fetch all the contents of the drop-down list.
- Validate if a particular entry exists in the drop-down.
- Fetch the number of items in the drop-down.
- Select a particular option in the drop-down.
- De-select a particular option in the drop-down.

We will only see the example code for **Fetch all the contents of the drop-down list**. The script is as follows:

```
1.    describe('Traverse Country Dropdown', function () {
2.      before(browser => browser.navigateTo('http://practice.bpbonline.
      com/'));
3.      it('Traverse Country Dropdown in Register User Page', function
      (browser) {
4.        browser
5.          .useXpath() // Set locator strategy to XPath
6.          .click('link text', 'My Account') //click on My Account Link
7.          .click("//a[@id='tdb4']")//click on Continue button
8.          // Assert that the First Name input field is present
9.          .assert.elementPresent("//input[@name='firstname']")
10.         // Wait for the country dropdown to be visible
11.         .waitForElementVisible("//select[@name='country']", 5000)
12.         // Fetch all the options from the country dropdown using CSS selector
13.         .elements('css selector', 'select[name="country"] option',
      function (result) {
```

```
14.          result.value.forEach(function (element, index) {
15.            browser.getText(element, function (text) {
16.              console.log('Option ' + (index + 1) + ' : ' + text.
        value);
17.            });
18.          });
19.        });
20.      });
21.
22.    after(browser => browser.end());
23.  });
```

As we execute the preceding code, we will find all the contents, which are the names of countries along with their index, printed in the console output window. We will see the output for all countries; however, for the sake of brevity, a smaller screenshot is shared of the results:

Running Traverse Country Dropdown in Register User Page:

√ Testing if element <//input[@name='firstname']> is present (39ms)
√ Element <//select[@name='country']> was visible after 34 milliseconds.
Option 1 : Please Select
Option 2 : Afghanistan
Option 3 : Albania
Option 4 : Algeria
Option 5 : American Samoa
Option 6 : Andorra
Option 7 : Angola
Option 8 : Anguilla
Option 9 : Antarctica
Option 10 : Antigua and Barbuda

Figure 10.10: Output of the drop-down code

Next, we will discuss iFrames.

Understanding iFrames and automating them

The iframe HTML tag stands for inline frame. It helps us embed another HTML document inside the main html document. Prior to iframe, we had frame and frameset tags, which, HTML 5 onwards are no longer supported by browsers. However, you may come across web applications where iframe is used. Suppose we want to interact with the html document, inside the iframe document. For this, we need to switch to the iframe, and only then we can access the elements within that document. To work with iframe, we will use the internet Heroku app. Let us see an example:

1. Launch the application using this URL, **https://the-internet.herokuapp.com/ iframe**

Figure 10.11: iframe containing a wysiwyg editor

2. We will now inspect this page to see the underlying HTML content of this.

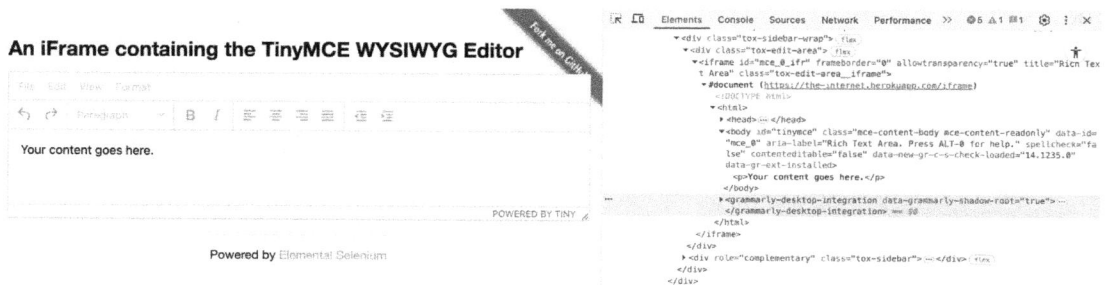

Figure 10.12: iframe example

3. To type anything inside the tiny editor, we first need to switch to the iframe. Once switched, we can access the HTML document and the elements inside the HTML document. If we do not switch and work directly, we will get an error that the element we are trying to search for is not there.

Look at the following script, which automates the above scenario:

```
1.  describe('Working with iFrames', function () {
2.    before(browser => browser.navigateTo('https://the-internet.
   herokuapp.com/iframe'));
3.    it('Working with iFrames', function (browser) {
4.      browser
5.        .useXpath() // Setting locator to be used as xpath for
   following commands
6.        .frame(0) // Switch to the first iframe on the page
7.        .waitForElementPresent("//*[@id='tinymce']", 30000) //
```

```
        Wait for the text area inside the iframe
8.           .getText("//*[@id='tinymce']", function (result) {
9.             console.log("Text inside iframe: " + result.value); //
    Log the text content
10.             this.assert.equal(result.value, "Your content goes
    here.", "Text content matches expected value."); // Assert the
    text content
11.           })
12.           .pause(3000)
13.           .frame(null) // Switch back to the main page
14.           .end(); // End the browser session
15.       });
16.     after(browser => browser.end());
17.   });
```

As the preceding script is executed, we will see the output where the text is fetched from the web element inside the iframe, which matches the expected. The output is as follows:

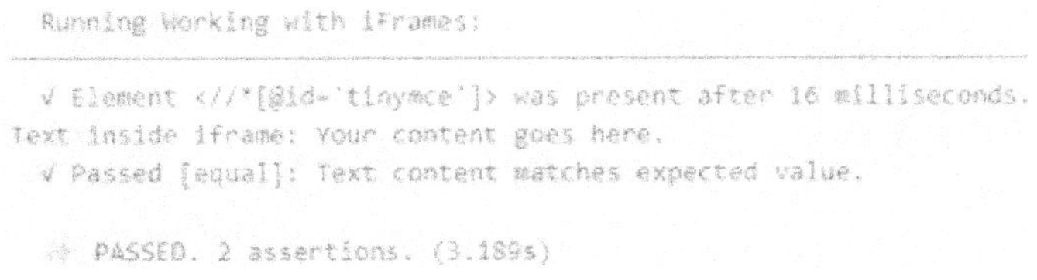

Figure 10.13: Output of iframe code execution

Understanding alerts and automating them

Alerts are JavaScript pop-ups that provide information to the end user and get a response from them. The alerts are of three kinds:

- **Alert pop-up**: The purpose of this alert is to simply provide information to the end user and make them aware. An example is:

https://the-internet.herokuapp.com/javascript_alerts

The first button in the following figure is an example of the Alert pop-up:

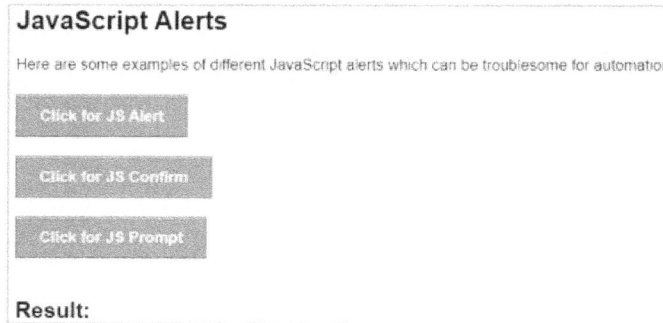

Figure 10.14: Example of alert types

Here, we have only one option, which is to press the **OK** button:

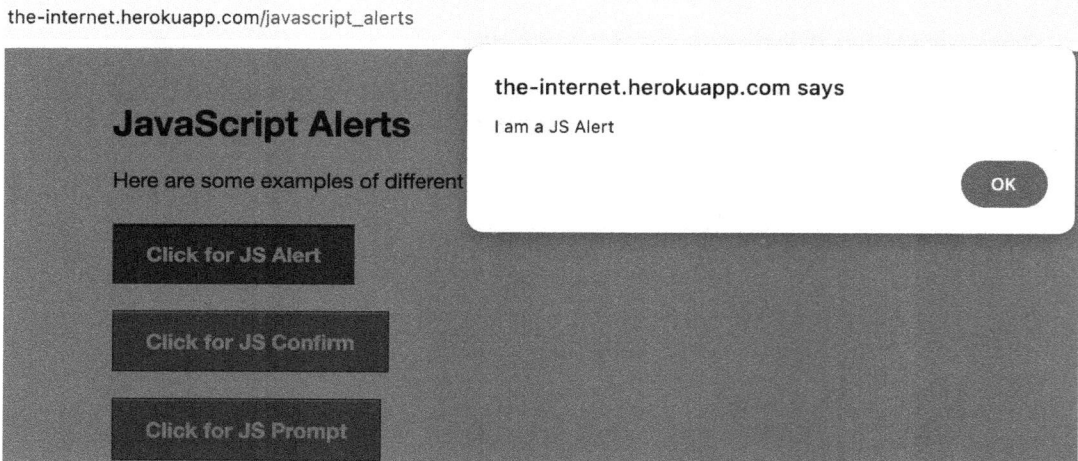

Figure 10.15: Example of alert popup

- **Confirm pop up**: The confirm pop up is a type of JavaScript alert where the end user is asked to confirm an action by clicking on either **OK** or **CANCEL**. An example is the second button shown in *Figure 10.11* of this chapter. Clicking on that shows us what is represented in the following figure:

the-internet.herokuapp.com/javascript_alerts

JavaScript Alerts

the-internet.herokuapp.com says

I am a JS Confirm

Here are some examples of different

OK   Cancel

Click for JS Alert

Click for JS Confirm

Click for JS Prompt

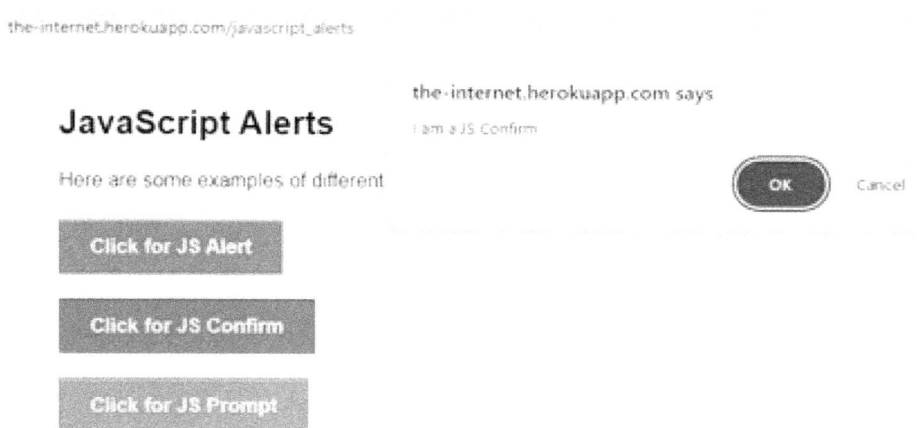

Figure 10.16: Confirm pop-up example

- **Prompt pop up**: The Prompt pop up is a type of JavaScript alert where the end user is prompted to provide data. Based on that, further processing can be done by the web application as per the business scenario. The third button in *Figure 10.11* shows an example of the prompt pop up. Clicking on it, we see the following:

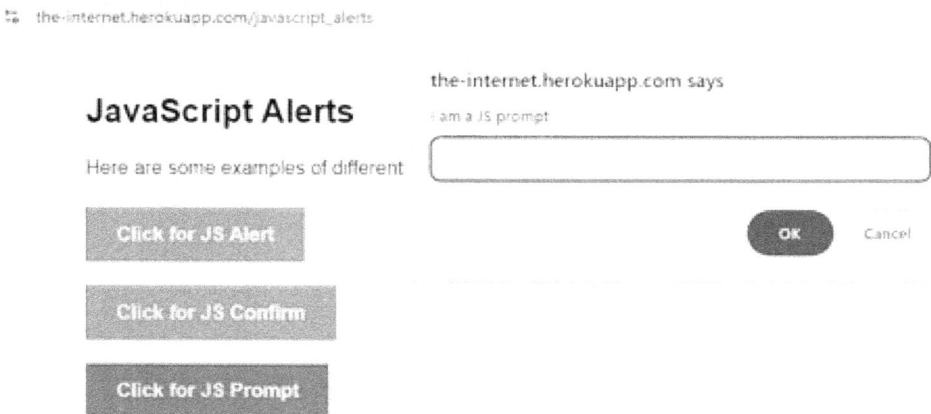

the-internet.herokuapp.com/javascript_alerts

JavaScript Alerts

the-internet.herokuapp.com says

I am a JS prompt

Here are some examples of different

OK   Cancel

Click for JS Alert

Click for JS Confirm

Click for JS Prompt

Figure 10.17: Prompt pop up example

Let us now, with the following script, learn how to automate them using Nightwatch:

```
1. describe('Handle Alerts', function() {
2.     before(browser => browser.navigateTo('https://the-
internet.herokuapp.com/javascript_alerts'));
3.     it('Handle Alerts', function(browser) {
4.         browser
```

```
5.          .useXpath() //setting locator to be used as xpath for
following commands
6.          //Example of Alert Javascript Popup
7.          .click("//button[contains(text(),'Click for JS
Alert')]")
8.          .pause(1000)
9.          .alerts.accept() // Accept the alert
10.             .pause(1000)
11.             .getText("//*[@id='result']", function (result)
{
12.             console.log("Text after alert: " + result.
value); // Log the text content
13.             browser.assert.equal(result.value, "You
successfully clicked an alert", "Text content matches expected
value."); // Assert the text content
14.             })
15.             //Example of Confirm Javascript Popup
16.             .click("//button[contains(text(),'Click for JS
Confirm')]")
17.             .pause(1000)
18.             .alerts.dismiss()
19.             .pause(1000)
20.             .getText("//*[@id='result']", function (result)
{
21.             console.log("Text after alert: " + result.
value); // Log the text content
22.             browser.assert.equal(result.value, "You
clicked: Cancel", "Text content matches expected value."); //
Assert the text content
23.             })
24.             //Example of Prompt Javascript Popup
25.             .click("//button[contains(text(),'Click for JS
Prompt')]")
26.             .pause(1000)
27.             .alerts.setText('hello world') // Set text for
the JS prompt
28.             .alerts.accept() // Accept the alert to submit
the text
29.             .pause(1000)
```

```
30.                    .getText("//*[@id='result']", function (result)
{
31.                        console.log("Text after alert: " + result.
value); // Log the text content
32.                        browser.assert.equal(result.value, "You
entered: hello world", "Text content matches expected value.");
// Assert the text content
33.                    })
34.                });
35.            after(browser => browser.end());
36.        });
```

As we execute the above script, we will see that one after the other three buttons of the page are clicked which cause the alerts to pop up one after the other. The required action is done to get the desired output, which is verified using assert.

The output which we see on the console is as follows:

```
Running Handle Alerts:

Text after alert: You successfully clicked an alert
  √ Passed [equal]: Text content matches expected value.
Text after alert: You clicked: Cancel
  √ Passed [equal]: Text content matches expected value.
Text after alert: You entered: hello world
  √ Passed [equal]: Text content matches expected value.

  ø PASSED. 3 assertions. (6.418s)
```

Figure 10.18: The output of alert handling code

Thus, we have seen three types of JavaScript alerts and how we can handle them.

Conclusion

In this chapter, we have seen tables, drop down, iframe, and alerts elements. We have also seen example scenarios that contain these elements and how, using Nightwatch, we can automate them.

In the next chapter, we will learn about some advanced concepts to handle browsers, work with mouse and keyboard, and fetch network logs.

Questions

1. How many rows does a web table contain?

2. What is a prompt JavaScript alert?

Join our book's Discord space

Join the book's Discord Workspace for Latest updates, Offers, Tech happenings around the world, New Release and Sessions with the Authors:

https://discord.bpbonline.com

CHAPTER 11

Browser Logs, Page Performance, Capture Screenshots, and Actions

In the previous chapter, we learned about the working of some advanced html elements, which are tables, frames, drop down, and alerts. We understood their function and how these elements can be automated for a scenario. In this chapter, we will cover some advanced concepts related to automation. While we automate an end application using Nightwatch, we may come across scenarios where we want to capture screenshots and advanced user actions that may need keyboard and mouse movements. We might also want to find the Page performance, capture browser logs or network requests to understand underlying functions and verify the behavior of the application.

Structure

In this chapter, we will discuss the following topics:

- Understanding browser logs and capturing them
- Understanding page performance and capturing them
- Capturing screenshots
- Understanding advanced user actions and automating them

Objectives

By the end of this chapter, you will be able to understand the browser logs and how to capture them. You will also understand page performance and network requests. You will be able to understand how we can capture screenshots using Nightwatch. Further, you will understand the advanced user actions with keyboard and mouse, for example, drag drop, or context menu handling. By the end of this chapter, you will learn how to automate them.

Understanding browser logs and capturing them

Browser logs, also known as network logs, record the activities and events that occur in the browser. They are generally used to capture front-end behavior of the web application or to understand any concerns raised by the add-on in the web application.

These logs are especially useful for the following:

- **Debugging JavaScript errors**: Detect and identify any script errors on the page.

- **Analyzing network requests**: See requests and responses exchanged between the client and server.

- **Monitoring console output**: Capture any `console.log`, `console.error`, or other console messages.

- **Ensuring compliance**: Identify potential security warnings or deprecated features used by the web application.

For example, let us first understand how to see the browser logs for an application. For this, we will use the chrome browser, and perform the following steps:

1. Open chrome browser, and launch the application using the URL: **https://practice. bpbonline.com/**

2. Once the application is opened, click *Ctrl + Shift + I*, it will open the **Chrome Dev Tools**. We select the **Network** tab on it. Please note this can change depending on the OS you are using.

3. Once we do the above, we will see the following:

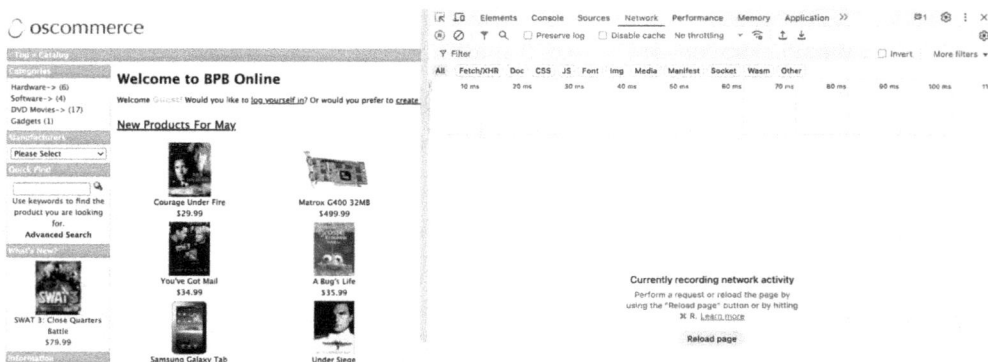

Figure 11.1: Chrome Dev Tools showing Network logs

4. Now, let us say we try to login to the application using wrong user credentials. As we do the activity, we will notice that the **Network** tab captures logs based on the user actions, as shown in the following figure:

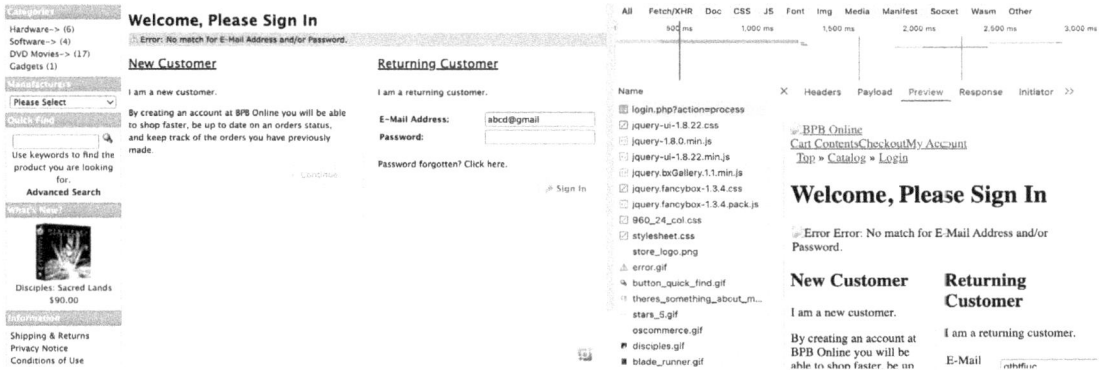

Figure 11.2: Logs captured for bad account login

5. Now, we can try another scenario in the same application where we can see it generating errors on the console log.

6. For this, we will try product search scenarios. Go to the homepage of the application and click on the manufacturers drop-down. Select **Fox** as shown in the following figure:

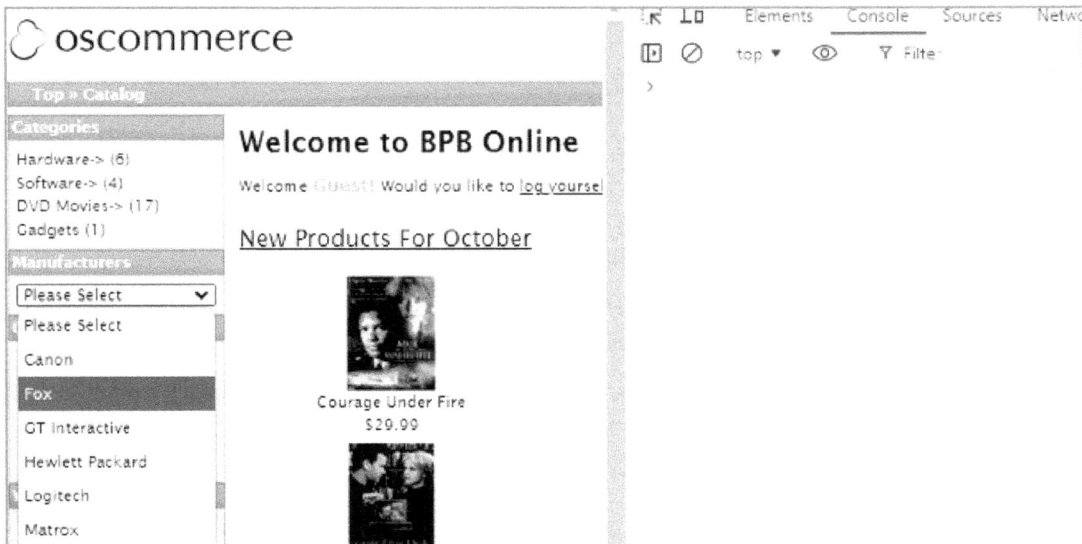

Figure 11.3: Product Search scenario for console logs

7. Select the first product shown, which is **Courage Under Fire**, as shown in the following figure:

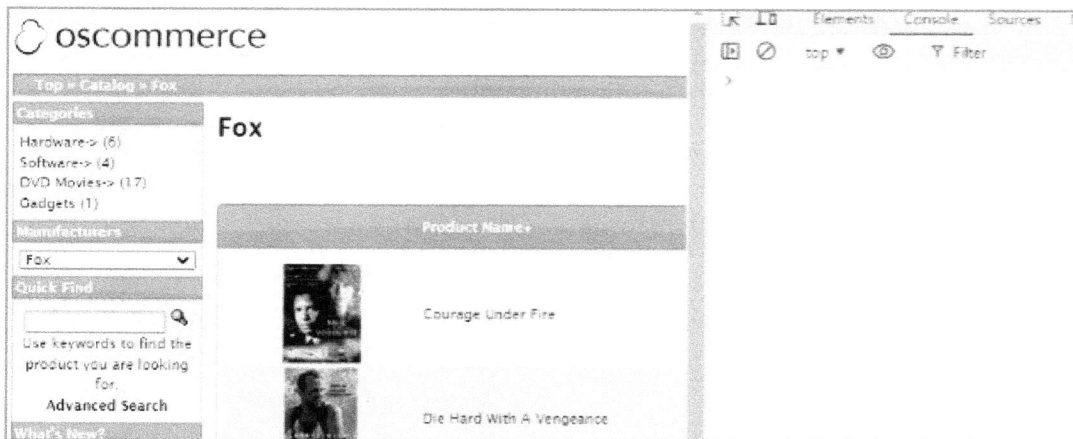

Figure 11.4: Choose the first product shown

8. As we do this, we can see an error generated in the console **log** of the **dev** tools, which informs that the page has requested some content over HTTP, which is blocked and should have been requested over HTTPS. The following screenshot illustrates that:

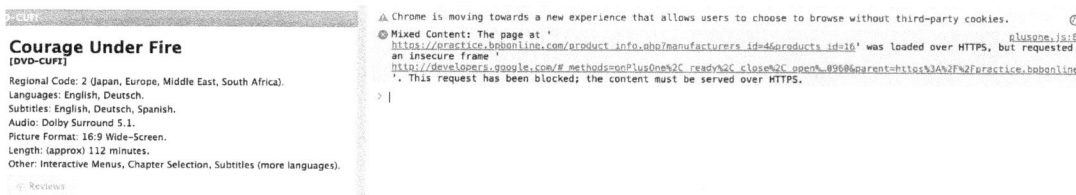

Figure 11.5: Error generated in console logs

Now, we will learn how to gather these console logs using Nightwatch as we automate the product search scenario in the application. For this, follow these steps:

Configure logging in **nightwatch.conf.js:** To capture browser logs, we need to add the following code in the **nightwatch.conf.json** file of the project:

```
webdriver: {
"log": {
  "browser": "ALL"
 }
},
```

Figure 11.6: Configure Nightwatch to capture browser logs

This configuration enables Nightwatch to capture all browser logs, including errors, warnings, and information logs.

1. Write the following script to search for a manufacturer Fox from the drop-down and then click on the product **Courage Under Fire**:

```
1. describe('Capture Network Logs', function () {
2.   before(browser => {
3.     browser.navigateTo('http://practice.bpbonline.com/');
4.   });
5.   it('Capture Network Logs', function (browser) {
6.     browser
7.       .useXpath() // Setting locator strategy to XPath for the
following commands
8.       .url('https://practice.bpbonline.com/index.php') //
Navigate to the specific page
9.       .click("//select[@name='manufacturers_id']") // Click on
the dropdown
10.      .click("//option[@value='4']") // Select the
option with value "Fox"
11.      .waitForElementVisible("//
a[contains(text(),'Courage Under Fire')]", 5000) // Wait for the
link to be visible
12.      .click("//a[contains(text(),'Courage Under
Fire')]") // Click on the link for the specific product
13.      .getLog('browser', function (logs) {
14.        logs.forEach(function (log) {
15.          console.log(log.message);
16.        });
17.      });
18.   });
19.   after(browser => {
20.     browser.end();
21.   });
22. });
```

In this script:

- **getLog('browser', callback)**: This method captures the browser logs, where 'browser' specifies the type of logs to retrieve. The **callback** function processes the logs.

- **console.log(log.message)**: Logs each browser log entry to the console for review.

2. As the above code executes, you will find in the output the same error messages of the console that we saw when we manually performed the scenario, as shown in the following figure:

```
[Capture Network Logs] Test Suite

Selenium Manager binary found at D:\WORK\BP9 PUBLICATIONS\NIGHTWATCH\TestProjectNwolc\node_modules\selenium-webdriver\bin\windows\se
enium-manager.exe
Driver path: C:\Users\HOME\.cache\selenium\chromedriver\win64\129.0.6668.89\chromedriver.exe
Browser path: C:\Program Files\Google\Chrome\Application\chrome.exe
  Using: chrome (129.0.6668.90) on WINDOWS.


Running Capture Network Logs:

  √ Element <//a[contains(text(),'Courage Under Fire')]> was visible after 331 milliseconds.
https://apis.google.com/js/plusone.js 81 Mixed Content: The page at 'https://practice.bpbonline.com/product_info.php?manufacturers_i
=4&products_id=16' was loaded over HTTPS, but requested an insecure frame 'http://developers.google.com/#_methods=onPlusOne%2C_ready
2C_close%2C_open%2C_resizeMe%2C_renderstart%2Concircled%2Cdrefresh%2Cerefresh%2Conload&id=I0_1728391405472&_gfid=I0_1728391405472&pa
ent=https%3A%2F%2Fpractice.bpbonline.com&pfname=&rpctoken=31095437'. This request has been blocked; the content must be served over
TTPS.
```

Figure 11.7: Output of the console logs

Thus, we saw how to capture the browser or network logs with Nightwatch as we automated the scenario.

Understanding page performance and capturing them

Page performance is a critical aspect of web development that directly impacts user experience. For test automation, monitoring page performance helps ensure that web applications load quickly, provide a seamless experience for end users, and bring a positive experience for your business. We can measure some key performance metrics using Nightwatch. For example:

- **Time to First Byte** (**TTFB**) is a crucial metric that informs about the time the server takes to respond to a user request.

- Page Load Time helps understand how much time it took the page to load completely.

- Another helpful metric is DOM Content Loaded, which measures the time it takes to load the page document object model, excluding the stylesheets and images.

For more such metric information, you can see this link:

https://www.metricfire.com/blog/top-8-web-application-performance-metrics/

Follow these steps to implement page performance with Nightwatch:

1. Set Nightwatch to capture performance metrics. The following needs to be added in the **nightwatch.conf.js** file.

```
webdriver: {
"log": {
  "browser": "ALL",
  "performance": "ALL"
  }
},
```

Figure 11.8: *Configure Nightwatch to capture performance logs*

This configuration ensures that Nightwatch can access performance logs from the browser.

2. Once this is done, we will now write code that will open the application having URL: **https://practice.bpbonline.com/index.php** on the Chrome browser. We will capture the Page Load time, the DOM Content Load time, and the TTFB. The script is as follows:

```
1.    describe('Capture Page Performance Metrics', function () {
2.      before(browser => {
3.        browser.navigateTo('http://practice.bpbonline.com/');
4.      });
5.      it('Capture Page Performance Metrics', function (browser) {
6.        browser
7.          .useXpath() // Setting locator strategy to XPath for the
      following commands
8.          .url('https://practice.bpbonline.com/index.php')
9.          .execute(function () {
10.           return JSON.stringify(window.performance.timing);
11.         }, [], function (result) {
12.           const performanceTiming = JSON.parse(result.value);
13.           const pageLoadTime = performanceTiming.loadEventEnd -
      performanceTiming.navigationStart;
14.           const domContentLoadedTime = performanceTiming.
      domContentLoadedEventEnd - performanceTiming.navigationStart;
15.           const timeToFirstByte = performanceTiming.responseStart
      - performanceTiming.navigationStart;
16.
17.           console.log('Page Load Time:', pageLoadTime);
18.           console.log('DOM Content Loaded Time:', domContentLoadedTime);
19.           console.log('Time to First Byte (TTFB):', timeToFirstByte);
20.         })
```

```
21.      });
22.      after(browser => {
23.        browser.end();
24.      });
25.    });
```

As the code will execute, we will find the metric captured and printed on the console, as shown in the following figure:

```
[Capture Page Performance Metrics] Test Suite

Selenium Manager binary found at D:\WORK\BPB PUBLICATIONS\NIGHTWATCH\TestProjectNWold\node_modules\sel
elenium-manager.exe
Driver path: C:\Users\HOME\.cache\selenium\chromedriver\win64\129.0.6668.89\chromedriver.exe
Browser path: C:\Program Files\Google\Chrome\Application\chrome.exe
  Using: chrome (129.0.6668.90) on WINDOWS.


  Running Capture Page Performance Metrics:

Page Load Time: 673
DOM Content Loaded Time: 385
Time to First Byte (TTFB): 357
```

Figure 11.9: Output of the page performance metric

Thus, we can capture some page performance metrics. Next, we will discuss capturing screenshots.

Capturing screenshots

When we automate a scenario using a tool like Nightwatch for testing purposes, it becomes crucial to empower the scripts written to capture screenshots. Screenshots provide more information on the behaviour of the application, which can help in debugging purposes while trying to fix a failed test scenario. In this section, we will understand how to capture screenshots using Nightwatch for a script. For this, we will take the login logout from the internet Heroku application.

1. Launch the application on browser using the URL: **https://the-internet.herokuapp. com/login**

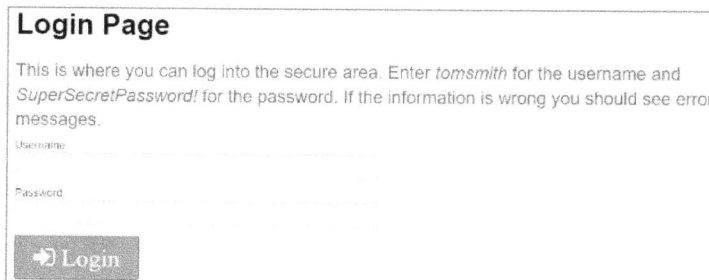

Login Page

This is where you can log into the secure area. Enter *tomsmith* for the username and *SuperSecretPassword!* for the password. If the information is wrong you should see error messages.

Username

Password

➔ Login

Figure 11.10: Login page of the internet Heroku application

2. Provide the username and password mentioned in the text and click on the **Login** button shown in the preceding figure to log into the application.

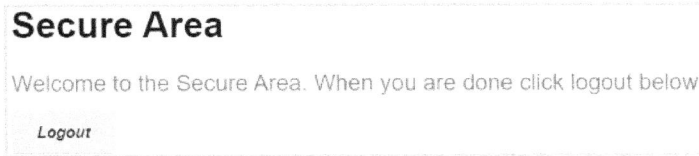

Figure 11.11: Logout button on the application

3. Once we click on logout, we are back to the home page of the application.

4. In this scenario, if we provide the wrong user credentials and attempt to login to the application, we will find an error message on the screen showing **Your username is invalid**, as shown in the following figure:

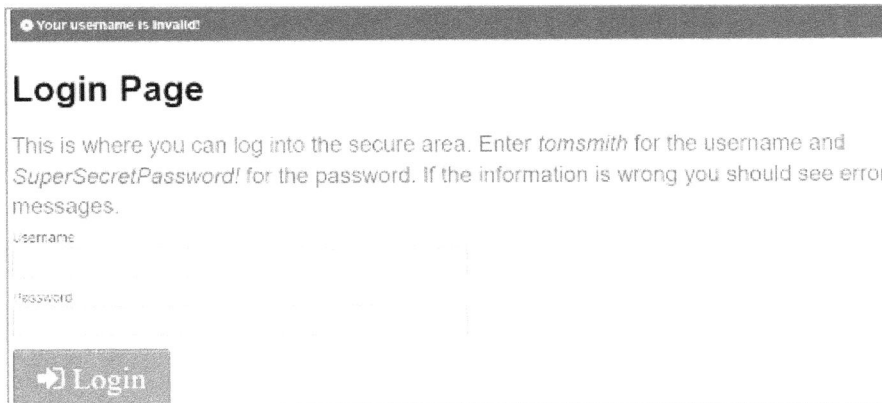

Figure 11.12: Error message on wrong user credential

We will now write a script that attempts login to the application with the wrong user credentials and capture the screenshot for it:

```
1.    describe('Capture Screenshot', function() {
2.      before(browser => browser.navigateTo('https://the-internet.
  herokuapp.com/login'));
3.      it('Capture Screenshot', function(browser) {
4.        browser
5.          .useXpath() // Setting locator strategy to XPath for the
  following commands
6.          .sendKeys("//input[@name='username']", 'tomsmith') //
  Enter the username
7.          .sendKeys("//input[@name='password']", 'wrongpwd') //
  Enter the password
```

```
8.              .click("//button[@type='submit']") // Click on the Login
   button
9.              .saveScreenshot('screenshots/badcredential-login.png') //
   Save the screenshot
10.             });
11.
12.        after(browser => browser.end());
13.     });
```

As we execute the code, we will see the wrong user credentials being entered, which generates the screen as shown in *Figure 11.12*. We can find the screenshot of this also captured. It will be in the **screenshots** folder inside the main project folder. The name of the file will be, **"screenshots/badcredential-login.png"**.

The following figure shows the image being captured and saved in the folder:

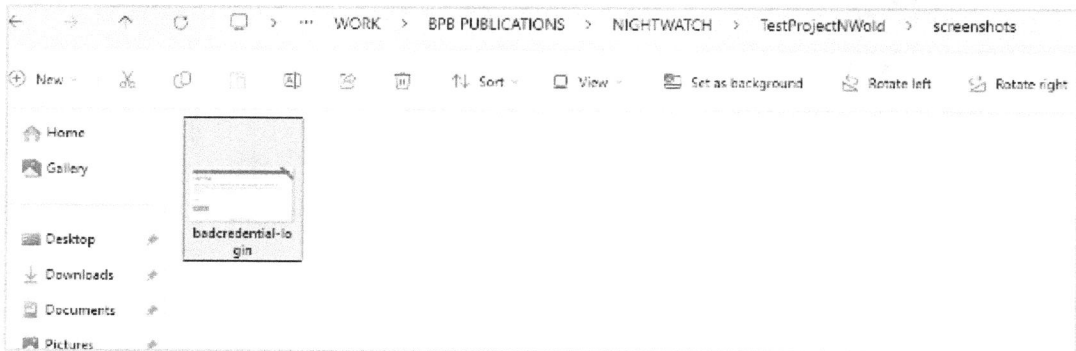

Figure 11.13: *Image captured by Nightwatch*

Next, we will learn about advanced user actions and how to automate it using Nightwatch.

Understanding advanced user actions and automating them

As we automate web applications, we can come across scenarios where advanced user actions are done. For example, double click on an element, drag-drop on a sidebar, work with the context menu, and other similar actions. More details on working with advanced or complex user actions with Nightwatch can be found at this link:

https://nightwatchjs.org/guide/writing-tests/write-complex-user-actions.html

These complex user gestures are based on the Actions API from the Selenium WebDriver. Let us look at the following table, where we list the commands that fall under this:

S. No.	Command	Meaning
1.	contextClick()	It right clicks with a mouse.
2.	doubleClick()	It double clicks an element.
3.	dragAndDrop()	It performs the drag and drop action on, or to an element. It clicks on the element in the center and then drags it to the element on which it has to be dropped.
4.	keyDown()	It performs the action of key down similar to what we see when we click that on a keyboard.
5.	keyUp()	It performs the action of key up similar to what we see on the keyboard when we click on the key.
6.	.pause()	Inserts a pause action before proceeding to the next action. It is generally used when we need to perform actions in a sequence.

Table 11.1: List of a few action commands

Let us see a scenario with the **contextMenu** command. For this, we will perform the following steps:

1. Launch the application on the browser using the URL: **https://the-internet. herokuapp.com/context_menu**

Context Menu

Context menu items are custom additions that appear in the right-click menu.

Right-click in the box below to see one called 'the-internet'. When you click it, it will trigger a JavaScript alert.

Figure 11.14: Context Menu application

2. As we now right-click on the box, we see a JavaScript alert popping up, as shown in the following figure:

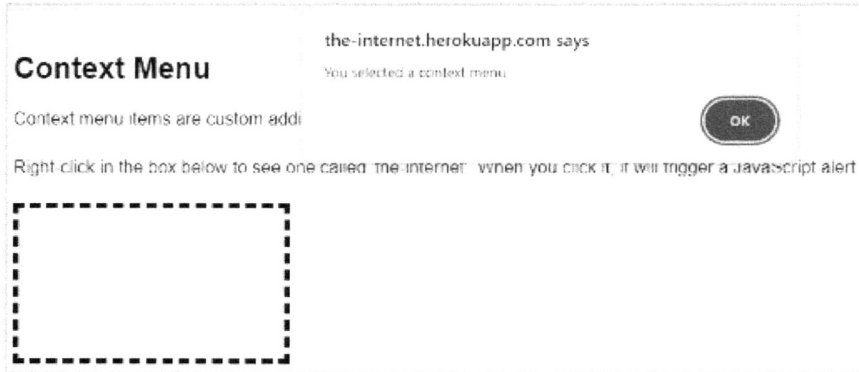

Figure 11.15: Right click event

3. We now need to click the **OK** button on the pop-up to handle it.

Let us write the script to automate the above steps using Nightwatch:

```
1.        describe('Automate Context Menu', function() {
2.          before(browser => browser.navigateTo('https://the-internet.
    herokuapp.com/context_menu'));
3.        it('Automate Context Menu', function(browser) {
4.            browser
5.            .useXpath() // Setting Locator strategy to XPath for the
    following commands
6.            .rightClick("//div[@id='hot-spot']") // Right click on the
    context menu
7.            .pause(2000) // Pause for 2 seconds
8.            .alerts.accept() // Accept the alert
9.            .pause(500)
10.            // Press the Escape key to close the modal or perform
    other actions
11.            .perform(() => {
12.              browser.sendKeys(browser.Keys.ESCAPE); // Simulates
    pressing the Escape key
13.              browser.pause(500);
14.            })
15.        });
16.        after(browser => browser.end());
17.        });
```

As we execute this code, we can see the right-click action being done, which results in the JavaScript alert to appear. We handle the alert by clicking on the **OK** button.

Let us see another example of working with action commands, where we first have to click on an element that brings change to the application state. So, we introduce a pause to wait for the state to be, and then proceed with the next action.

1. Launch the application on the browser using the URL: **https://the-internet. herokuapp.com/hovers**

Figure 11.16: Application for hover

2. As shown in the following figure, when we bring our mouse to hover over any image, we get extra information on the screen. We get a link called View profile, which is otherwise not visible. Then, we can click on View profile to learn more about the user.

Figure 11.17: Click on the View profile link which appears as mouse is hovered over image 2

3. When we click on the **View profile**, it will take us to the page for user 2. Since this is not implemented, we find the page saying **Not Found**.

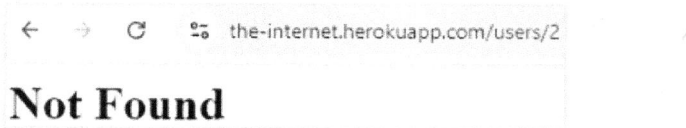

Not Found

Figure 11.18: Page after click on View profile

4.   Let us automate this with Nightwatch:

```
1. describe('Working with Action Ticks', function() {
2.   before(browser => {
3.     browser.navigateTo('https://the-internet.herokuapp.com/
hovers');
4.   });
5.
6.   it('Working with Action Ticks', function(browser) {
7.     browser
8.       .useXpath() // Set locator strategy to XPath for
subsequent commands
9.       .click("//*[@id='content']/div/div[2]/img") // Hover over
the second image at (0,0)
10.      .pause(2000) // Pause for 2 seconds to allow the hover
effect to be visible
11.      .click('link text', 'View profile')// Click on Continue
link
12.      .pause(2000); // Pause for 2 seconds to observe the result
13.   });
14.
15.   after(browser => browser.end());
16. });
```

5.   Thus, as we execute this code, we will find the image 2 being clicked, which makes the View profile link appear, and we finally click on it.

In this section, we learned about advanced or complex user actions and how to handle them with Nightwatch.

Conclusion

In this chapter, we saw various topics for advanced automation. We saw and understood browser logs, page performance, capturing screenshots, and complex user action. These advanced concepts help us automate more complex scenarios with Nightwatch and gather more information on the application behavior as we automate it.

In the next chapter, we will discuss object management of automation projects using the concept of page objects.

Questions

1. Explain the contextMenu() command in Nightwatch.

2. What is the purpose of capturing browser logs?

Answers

1. The contextMenu() command in Nightwatch helps right-click on an element.

2. Capturing browser logs helps us validate whether an action is performed at the server level by capturing logs.

Join our book's Discord space

Join the book's Discord Workspace for Latest updates, Offers, Tech happenings around the world, New Release and Sessions with the Authors:

https://discord.bpbonline.com

CHAPTER 12
Page Objects

In the previous chapter, we learned about advanced automation concepts like browser logs, page performance, capture screenshots, and actions. We also learned how and where these concepts are useful and how to automate them using Nightwatch and make them a part of the test script. In this chapter, we will learn about Page Objects.

Page Object was first defined by *Martin Fowler* in 2013. Its documentation can be read here: **https://martinfowler.com/bliki/PageObject.html**. Page Objects are crucial design patterns that one should adopt when writing test scripts. It allows us to create a separation layer between the application under test and the script being created to automate the process. By adding this layer of abstraction, we can separate the application object information prone to change as it develops from the test logic. In this chapter, we will understand what Page Objects are, how to implement them in our test script, and how they elevate our test design and make it more robust.

Structure

This chapter will have the following sections:

- Understanding Page Objects
- Implementing Page Object for test automation
- Advantages of Page Object Design Pattern

Objectives

After completing this chapter, you will be able to understand Page Objects and how to implement them for the automation project. You will also understand the benefit of Page Object Design Pattern and create robust automation code. Page Object Design Pattern also helps in code maintenance in the long run, as we add a layer of abstraction when implementing Page Object. In this chapter, you will understand it better and how it can be implemented.

Understanding Page Objects

In *Chapter 5, Identifying Elements,* we understood the concept of selectors. We saw that the html element we would want to interact with for automation can be identified by the html information associated with it. Here, we also need to understand that as the application undergoes development, the html information associated with the html element can undergo change. If it undergoes change, it will impact all the automation scripts that are created where that object is used. If the impact is on more than one object, we need to be aware of the number of scripts that can be impacted. Also, this can happen with every development change being done on the application.

Since the test automation scripts we are creating consist of the object information, any change in the object information will lead to changes in the script. The more a script is prone to change, the more it will be prone to error. The way to avoid this is to add a layer of abstraction. The purpose of adding the layer of abstraction is to make the test scripts more robust and maintainable. We can achieve this by using the Page Object Design Pattern.

Page Object, introduced by *Martin Fowler* defines a Page Object as wrapping an HTML page, or fragment, with an application-specific API, allowing one to manipulate page elements without digging around in the HTML. Another point that Martin mentions, and is crucial to understand is that, while creating Page Objects, we only create Page Objects for relevant objects in a page. An HTML page of interest can have multiple HTML elements on it. However, not all are relevant for the various business scenarios that we would want to test. So, when we create Page Objects, we only consider the HTML elements needed for our test scenarios.

The making of Page Objects could be different as per your test architecture. Some may decide to include validation within the Page Object code, whereas others may validate in the test script. Both these approaches are okay, and depend largely on the approach the test framework is taking. For more information on Page Objects, follow this link:

https://martinfowler.com/bliki/PageObject.html

Next, we will take an example from our application and see how to create Page Objects for it with Nightwatch.

Implementing Page Object for test automation

In this section, we will understand, with the help of example, how to implement Page Objects for the application under test. The application we will consider for this is the *Practice BPB Application*. The URL of the application is **https://practice.bpbonline.com/index.php**. We will take the scenario of login logout. Let us write down the steps for it, and start giving the pages' names as we navigate across them to complete the action of login logout:

1. Home page:

    a. Launch the application on a browser with the URL: **https://practice.bpbonline.com/index.php**

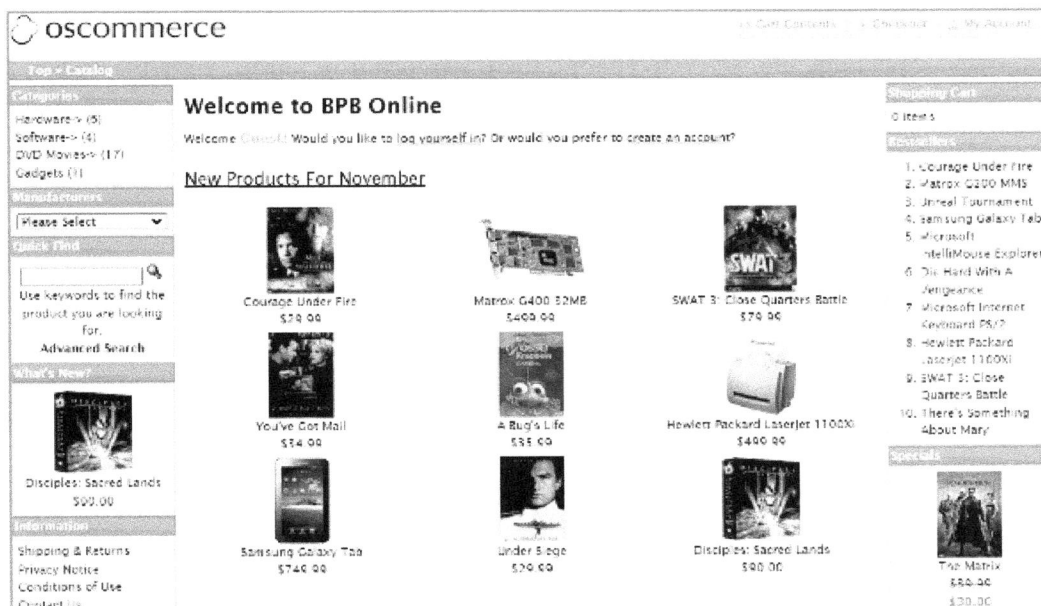

Figure 12.1: Home page of the application

    b. Click on the **My Account** link.

2. Login page:

    a. Type register username and password.

    b. Then, click on the **Sign In** button to login to the application, as shown in the following figure:

Figure 12.2: Login Page of the application

3. My Accounts page:

   a. Once logged in as a verified user, we can see the account-related information. This page allows us to change the password if required, view the orders the user has made, etc.

   b. Once the user is logged in, we can see the **Log Off** link, which we want to click to proceed to logging off from the application.

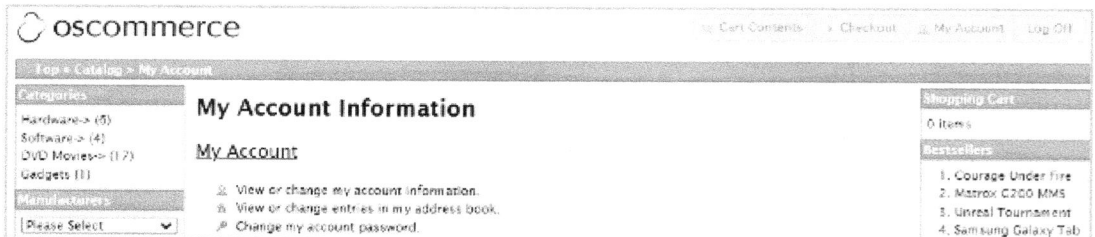

Figure 12.3: My Account page with Log Off link

4. Log Off page:

   a. When we click on the **Log Off** link, we reach this page. This page contains a **Continue** button, which we need to click to finally log off from the application.

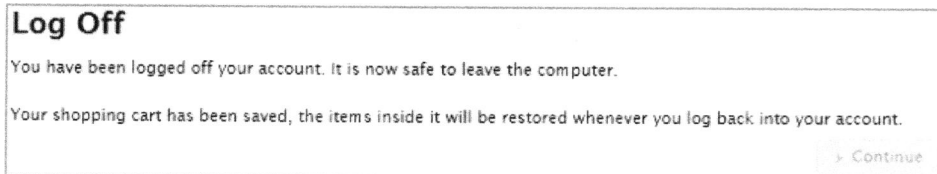

Figure 12.4: Log Off page with continue button

   b. On clicking the **Continue** button, we are back on the home page.

As you may have noticed, we traversed various pages in our application, and on each of these pages, we have many objects. However, we only need a few from each page to work on. The following table shows the pages and objects needed for our test scenario of login logout:

S. No.	Page name	Objects
1.	Home page	My Account: Link
2.	Login page	Email address: TextBox
		Password: TextBox
		Sign in: Button
3.	My Accounts page	Log Off: Link
4.	Log Off page	Continue: Link

Table 12.1: Page names with objects

Note: In the preceding table, we have currently only considered adding the objects we need for the scenario of login logout.

For example, we want to automate the scenario of changing the password for an account. This can be done once you are logged in to the application. In the **My Accounts** page, *Figure 12.3* shows a **Change my account password** link. So, when trying to automate this scenario, we can add the Page Object of this link in the existing My Account page in our code. We do not create multiple Page Objects of a single page; rather, we add objects to any existing page based on its presence in the application.

Coming back to our scenario of login logout, we can see from *Table 12.1*, there are four pages we will traverse:

- Home page
- Login page
- My Accounts page
- Log Off page

In each of these pages, we have marked the objects that we need, to perform the login logout action. Each object is an HTML object, and in *Table 12.1*, we have mentioned along with the object name, the type of HTML object it is. One Page Object can be used by more than one test script, based on the scenario we are creating to test. In the same manner, a test script can have Page Objects from various pages as we traverse through the application to complete the business scenario.

For the example above, login logout, let us see the representation of Page Objects and test script:

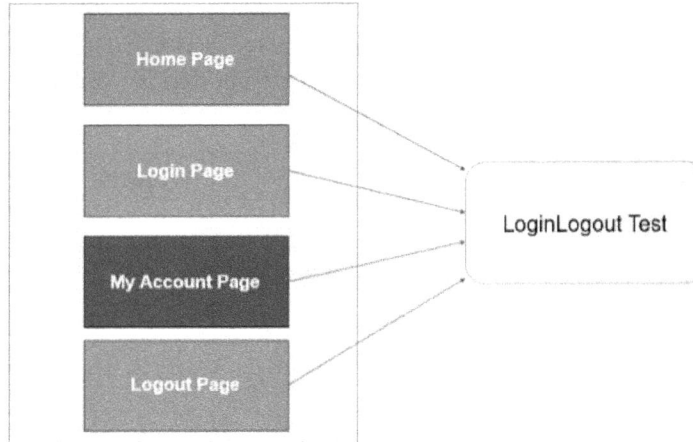

Figure 12.5: Page Object Model for login logout

Based on the preceding figure, we will now create the Page Objects and the test script for the login logout scenario.

Main script

Look at the following code:

```
/*
  Login Logout with Page Object Model
*/
describe('Login Logout using Page Objects', function() {
  const homepage = browser.page.bpbpractice.homepage(); // home Page Object
  before(async () => homepage.navigate());
  it('Login Logout BPB Application', function(browser) {
    homepage.click('@myAccountLink')
    const loginpage = browser.page.bpbpractice.loginpage(); // Login Page
Object
    loginpage.assert.elementPresent("@username_txtbox") //asserting element
presence
    loginpage.login("bpb@bpb.com","bpb@123")
    //Logout Page Object
    const logoutpage = browser.page.bpbpractice.logoutpage(); // Logout
Page Object
    logoutpage.assert.elementPresent("@logoutLink") //asserting element
presence
    logoutpage.logout()
```

```
  });
  after(async (browser) => browser.quit());
});
```

Home page

The Page Object Model code is as follows:

```
/**
 * A Nightwatch Page Object. The Page Object name is the filename.
 *
 * Usage:
 *    browser.page.bpbpractice.homepage()
 *
 * For more information on working with Page Objects, see:
 *    https://nightwatchjs.org/guide/concepts/page-object-model.html
 *
 */
const homepage={
  clickMyAccount() {
      this.waitForElementVisible('@myAccountLink', 1000)
      .click('@myAccountLink');
      this.pause(1000);
      return this; // for command-chaining
  },
};
module.exports = {
  url: 'https://practice.bpbonline.com/',
  commands: [
    homepage
  ],
  elements: {
    myAccountLink: {
      selector: '//a[@id="tdb3"]',
      locateStrategy: 'xpath',
      index: 0
    },
  }
};
```

Login page

The Object Model code is as follows:

```
/**
 * A Nightwatch Page Object. The Page Object name is the filename.
 *
 * Usage:
 *   browser.page.bpbpractice.loginpage()
 *
 * For more information on working with Page Objects, see:
 *   https://nightwatchjs.org/guide/concepts/page-object-model.html
 *
 */
const loginAccount={
  login(username,password) {
    this.typeUsername(username),
    this.typePassword(password)
    this.clickSignInBtn()
  },
    typeUsername(str) {
      this.waitForElementVisible('@username_txtbox', 1000)
      .sendKeys('@username_txtbox',str)
      this.pause(1000);
      return this; // for command-chaining
    },
    typePassword(str) {
      this.waitForElementVisible('@password_txtbox', 1000)
      .sendKeys('@password_txtbox',str)
      this.pause(1000);
      return this; // for command-chaining
    },
  clickSignInBtn() {
    this.waitForElementVisible('@signin_btn', 1000)
    .click('@signin_btn');
    this.pause(1000);
    return this; // for command-chaining
  },
```

```
};
module.exports = {
  url: 'https://practice.bpbonline.com/',
  commands: [
    loginAccount
  ],
  elements: {
    username_txtbox: {
      selector: '//input[@name="email_address"]',
      locateStrategy: 'xpath',
      index: 0
    },
    password_txtbox: {
      selector: '//input[@name="password"]',
      locateStrategy: 'xpath',
      index: 0
    },
    signin_btn: {
      selector: '//button[@id="tdb5"]',
      locateStrategy: 'xpath',
      index: 0
    },

  }
};
```

Logout page

The Object Model code is as follows:

```
/**
 * A Nightwatch Page Object. The Page Object name is the filename.
 *
 * Usage:
 *    browser.page.bpbpractice.logoutpage()
 *
 * For more information on working with Page Objects, see:
 *    https://nightwatchjs.org/guide/concepts/page-object-model.html
 *
```

```
*/
const logoutAccount={
  logout() {
    this.clickLogout(),
    this.clickContinue()
  },
    clickLogout() {
      this.waitForElementVisible('@logoutLink', 1000)
      .click('@logoutLink')
      this.pause(1000);
      return this; // for command-chaining
    },
    clickContinue() {
      this.waitForElementVisible('@continueLink', 1000)
      .click('@continueLink')
      this.pause(1000);
      return this; // for command-chaining
    },
  };
module.exports = {
  url: 'https://practice.bpbonline.com/',
  commands: [
    logoutAccount
  ],
  elements: {
    logoutLink: {
      selector: '//a[@id="tdb4"]',
      locateStrategy: 'xpath',
      index: 0
    },
    continueLink: {
      selector: '//a[@id="tdb4"]',
      locateStrategy: 'xpath',
      index: 0
    },
  }
};
```

The preceding code shows us three Page Object model pages: **homepage.js**, **loginpage.js**, and **logoutpage.js**. We will find that in each of the individual Page Objects code, we have declared the elements that we will encounter on those pages and described the function associated with it. For example, on the home page, we have the My Account link. How will we identify it? The following code snippet reflects that:

```
elements: {
  myAccountLink: {
    selector: '//a[@id="tdb3"]',
    locateStrategy: 'xpath',
    index: 0
  },
```

Figure 12.6: My Account link description in Page Object code

We can find from the preceding information that the My Account link will be identified using **xpath** with the value being – **'//a[@id="tbd3"]'**. Now, we will have a look at the code snippet where we define the action we will perform, which is click. We define this with the help of the following function:

```
const homepage={
  clickMyAccount() {
    this.waitForElementVisible('@myAccountLink', 1000)
    .click('@myAccountLink');
    this.pause(1000);
    return this; // for command-chaining
  },
};
```

Figure 12.7: My Account link action defined as function

Now, when we call this in the main code, we will first need to create an object of the homepage and then call the function. The following code snippet shows that:

```
describe('Login Logout using Page Objects', function() {
  const homepage = browser.page.bpbpractice.homepage(); // home page object
  before(async () => homepage.navigate());
  it('Login Logout BPB Application', function(browser) {
    homepage.click('@myAccountLink')
```

Figure 12.8: Creating object of the homepage and calling function

In a similar manner, we can find for other Page Object code files of loginpage.js and logoutpage.js. As discussed earlier in the chapter, the many benefits of creating and using Page Objects for designing automation code can be witnessed in this example. As the application evolves and the locator information for any element changes, you only need to update it in its corresponding Page Object file, and the update will automatically reflect wherever that Page Object is used. There are various benefits of the Page Object model, and it is a crucial design pattern that should be adopted in your test automation project.

Advantages of Page Object Design Pattern

The Page Object Design Pattern simplifies automated testing by isolating UI interactions into dedicated classes. This separation allows test scripts to concentrate on business logic rather than getting bogged down with interface details. As a result, any changes in the UI only necessitate updates in the relevant Page Objects, rather than modifications across multiple tests. This approach not only boosts code maintainability and reusability but also enhances the clarity and scalability of the testing framework.

Conclusion

In this chapter, we learned what Page Objects are, how they are created in Nightwatch, and the advantages of using them in the code for test automation. We created a Page Object for the home page, login page, and logout page, and then called them in the main code to explain how to implement them. On similar lines, you can first find the common pages, objects, and functions for your application and use this design pattern for automation.

In the next chapter, we will learn how to manage data in Excel and CSV files and create scripts around it to data drive the tests.

Questions

1. Who introduced the concept of Page Objects?

2. Are there other design patterns that can be explored besides Page Objects, which are commonly used in test automation?

3. Should we create Page Objects for all pages in the application?

Answers

1. Martin Fowler

2. Yes, like Factory Pattern.

3. This depends on the approach to the test automation architecture you want to build.

CHAPTER 13
Managing Data Using Excel and CSV Files

In the previous chapter, we learned about managing objects through the concept of Page Objects. This is important when you are automating an application. By implementing Page Objects, one is able to create a layer of abstraction where, from the actual test script, the locator information, which helps in identifying the objects, is hidden. At the same time, we are able to achieve modularity in the code and make it more robust to changes to the application. So as the application is developing and the object locator information changes, we do not have to make changes at all code places where we have used the object, as before using the object we first need to identify it. This is taken care of by the Page Objects and helps with overall maintainability of the automation code. In a similar manner, as we have managed the objects, we should manage the data for automation. Data, which is crucial to automation code, should be managed outside the test scripts. Activities like reading, writing, and generating data should be done with the help of data libraries.

In this chapter, we will explore how to read, write, and manage data for two data sources, i.e., csv and excel. The data sources could be in other formats as well, like XML, JSON and the concepts which we use to read for csv and excel can be further implemented for other data sources. Let us now see why and how data for automation is crucial and how to handle it for the project.

Structure

This chapter will have the following sections:

- Introduction to data
- Introduction to data sources
- Read and write CSV files
- Read and write Excel files

Objectives

By the end of this chapter, you will be able to understand what data is, and how it is important for the test automation project. We will explore data sources and their types. We will then move on to exploring how we can read and write data in the csv file and Excel file.

Introduction to data

Data is a collection of words, facts, numbers, and other similar useful information. It can be structured, unstructured, or semi-structured. Processed data brings information, a crucial aspect of test automation. Generally, for any test automation project, we may have to create our test data, maintain and manage it. In many scenarios, new data needs to be generated, which, once used in workflows might need to be discarded. Data should also be similar to the ones we see in production. Keeping all such aspects in mind, we need to build a strategy to manage test data outside test scripts.

Introduction to data sources

Data source is a place where the data is stored to be used further. For example, an Excel workbook, a CSV file, a database, JSON files, etc. The data stored in the data source can be structured or unstructured depending on the way it is managed and has to be used. The data source can be located in the location where you plan to execute your test automation scripts or in an entirely different location, and you can then access it. In most situations, data is stored in other locations. Sometimes, to ensure less delay in the test automation scripts we can decide to store data locally. Data is also generated by the test automation scripts, used, and then discarded as a test suite executes. Whatever strategy you use to handle data for your test automation project is a decision you need to take based on the requirements and expertise available within the team.

Read and write CSV files

A **comma separated value** (**CSV**) file is a plain file which stores data in tabular format. The values in a CSV file are comma-separated; we then consider each value as a column.

We can also use other delimiters instead of commas to separate values from each other. The delimiter could be a tab, a semicolon, or a custom one. CSV files are a good option to store information and retrieve it from them. However, they lack features to format the data since they are plain data files. Many times, for test automation projects, we store data in csv files and use them. In this section, we will understand how to write a csv file and read information from it. Once we have learned it, we will understand how to use it in our test automation script.

Let us have a look at how a sample CSV file looks with the following figure:

```
Title,Author,ISBN13,Pages
1984,George Orwell,978-0451524935,268
Animal Farm,George Orwell,978-0451526342,144
Brave New World,Aldous Huxley,978-0060929879,288
Fahrenheit 451,Ray Bradbury,978-0345342966,208
Jane Eyre,Charlotte Brontë,978-0142437209,532
Wuthering Heights,Emily Brontë,978-0141439556,416
Agnes Grey,Anne Brontë,978-1593083236,256
Walden,Henry David Thoreau,978-1420922615,156
Walden Two,B. F. Skinner,978-0872207783,301
"Eats, Shoots & Leaves",Lynne Truss,978-1592400874,209
```

Figure 13.1: Sample CSV file

The preceding image shows an example of the CSV file. We can see that:

- The first row describes the column names for which there exists data from the second row onwards. The first row's column names are: **Title**, **Author**, **ISBN13**, **Pages**.
- The CSV file describes the meta information about a book.
- The following rows have actual data which contain the title of the book, author name, **ISBN13** number and finally, the page count of the book.

To work with CSV files, we will use the **fs** module, (the default module with Node) to work with files. You can find information about this module here: **https://nodejs.org/api/fs.html**, and a good document to understand the working with it is:

https://www.w3schools.com/nodejs/nodejs_filesystem.asp

Using this, we will learn how to create and write a CSV file. Further, we will learn how to read the content from the CSV file to pass to our test automation script.

Writing CSV files

To write a CSV file, we first have to create the file. Once the file is created we can use either the write method or append. The write method will overwrite the file if one exists, and the append method will add data to the existing file. Let us see with the following code example how to create a CSV file. The file we created will be with the user details to be used for Log in to the BPB practice application. The following is the code for it:

```
const fs = require("fs");
const data = `
username,password
bpb@bpb.com,bpb@123
error@error.com,error@123
`;
fs.writeFile("data.csv", data, "utf-8", (err) => {
  if (err) console.log(err);
  else console.log("Data saved");
});
```

This will create a file called **data.csv** in the system. If we open the file, we will see the following contents:

```
username,password
bpb@bpb.com,bpb@123
error@error.com,error@123
```

Figure 13.2: data.csv file contents

Reading CSV files

Once we have the data file generated, we will look at the code that we can use to read the CSV file. Follow this code for the same:

```
const fs = require("fs");
fs.createReadStream("data.csv", { encoding: "utf-8" })
  .on("data", (chunk) => {
    console.log(chunk);
  })
  .on("error", (error) => {
    console.log(error);
  });
```

When we execute the preceding code, we will see the following output:

```
C:\Program Files\nodejs\node.exe .\nightwatch\examples\codeexamplesbook\chapter13-readcsvfile.js

username,password
bpb@bpb.com,bpb@123
error@error.com,error@123
```

Figure 13.3: Output of read CSV file code

In the next section, we will create a script to perform the login-logout action by reading and using data from a CSV file.

Creating login logout with CSV data

We now have the code available for both, writing the file and reading the contents. Next, we will create a login logout script to read data from the csv file and pass it to the underlying test automation script for login. The login logout code will be executed as many times as there are rows in the file. Let us have a look at it.

To keep things simple and focused, we will see the implementation without using Page Object models or error handling. These could be later added to the script and will move towards framework design, which is currently out of scope for the beginner book.

The first part of the problem is creating a **CSV data file** for our project. The csv file contents are as follows:

```
nightwatch > examples > codeexamplesbook > ▨ data.csv > ☐ data
1    email,password
2    bpb@bpb.com,bpb@123
3    someone@example.com,junk
```

Figure 13.4: Data file with user and password details for login

- The second file is **dataReader**, where we will create a function that will read data from the CSV file and return us an array of data. This array of data can then be used in the file which performs the actual action of login logout on the application. Let us look at the code of the **dataReader** file:

```
// dataReader.js
const fs = require('fs');
/**
 * Reads data from a CSV file and returns a Promise that resolves to
an array of objects.
 * The first line in the CSV is assumed to be a header row (e.g.
"email,password").
 *
 * Example CSV:
 *    email,password
 *    bpb@bpb.com,bpb@123
 *      *
 * @param {string} filePath - path to your CSV file
 * @returns {Promise<Array<Object>>} - e.g. [ {email: "bpb@bpb.com",
password: "bpb@123"}, ... ]
 */
```

```javascript
function readDataFromCSV(filePath) {
  return new Promise((resolve, reject) => {
    let fileContent = '';
    // Create read stream with UTF-8 encoding
    fs.createReadStream(filePath, { encoding: 'utf-8' })
      // `data` event fires whenever a new chunk of data is read
      .on('data', (chunk) => {
        fileContent += chunk;
      })
      // `end` event fires when the entire file has been read
      .on('end', () => {
        // Split the CSV text into lines
        const lines = fileContent.trim().split('\n');
        // The first line is the header row
        const headers = lines[0].split(',');
        const rows = [];
        // Process each subsequent line
        for (let i = 1; i < lines.length; i++) {
          const rowData = lines[i].split(',');
          const rowObject = {};
          // Build an object using the headers as keys
          headers.forEach((header, index) => {
            rowObject[header.trim()] = rowData[index] ?
rowData[index].trim() : '';
          });
          rows.push(rowObject);
        }
        resolve(rows);
      })
      // `error` event if something goes wrong reading the file
      .on('error', (error) => {
        reject(error);
      });
  });
}
module.exports = { readDataFromCSV };
```

The preceding code, as mentioned, will read the data from the CSV file and store the details in the array. This function will return a data array, which can then be passed into the login function.

- The third file, which performs the login and logout on the application using Nightwatch, is as follows:

```
const { readDataFromCSV } = require('./dataReader.js');
describe('Login Logout BPB', function() {
  let credentials = [];
  // Load CSV data before starting the test
  before(function(browser, done) {
    readDataFromCSV('D:\\WORK\\BPB PUBLICATIONS\\NIGHTWATCH\\
BPBNightWatchProject\\nightwatch\\examples\\codeexamplesbook\\data.
csv')  // <-- Make sure your CSV file name/path is correct
      .then(data => {
        credentials = data;
        done();  // Tell Nightwatch we're done with async setup
      })
      .catch(err => {
        done(err); // Pass any error to Nightwatch
      });
  });

  it('Login Logout with Data', function(browser) {
    credentials.forEach((row, index) => {
      browser
        .useXpath()
        .navigateTo('http://practice.bpbonline.com/')
        .click('link text', 'My Account')
        .setValue("//input[@name='email_address']", row.email)
        .setValue("//input[@name='password']", row.password)
        .click("//button[@id='tdb5']")
        .assert.elementPresent("//*[contains(text(),'Log Cff')]")
        .click('link text', 'Log Off')
        .click('link text', 'Continue')
        .assert.not.elementPresent("//*[contains(text(),'Log
Off')]")
    });
  });
  // Close the browser after the tests finish
  after(browser => browser.end());
});
```

In the preceding code, we can see that we call the function **readDataFromCSV(filepath)** and pass the file path to it. It reads data from the csv file and creates an array named credentials. The array is then iterated using the **forEach** method, and inside the loop, we have called the steps to perform the login and logout action. We need to note the following two commands:

```
.setValue("//input[@name='email_address']", row.email)

.setValue("//input[@name='password']", row.password)
```

In these two commands, instead of passing the actual data, we pass **row.email**, and **row. password**. These, at the time of execution, will be replaced by the data present in the file, and the whole loop will iterate as many times as many lines are there in the file. So, when you execute the code, it will run twice. The first line in the **data.csv** file is for valid user details, and the second line is for invalid user details. Hence, the first iteration will pass, but when it tries to execute the second iteration, it will fail.

The output of execution will look as follows:

```
PS D:\WORK\BPB PUBLICATIONS\NIGHTWATCH\BPBNightWatchProject> npx nightwatch
.\nightwatch\examples\codeexamplesbook\chapter13-loginDataTest.js
[Login Logout BPB] Test Suite

────────────────────────────────────────────────────────────────

: Starting ChromeDriver on port 9515...
i Connected to ChromeDriver on port 9515 (638ms).
  Using: chrome (131.0.6778.266) on WINDOWS.
  Running Login Logout with Data:

────────────────────────────────────────────────────────────────

  ─────────────────────────────────

  √ Testing if element <//*[contains(text(),'Log Off')]> is present (27ms)
  √ Testing if element <//*[contains(text(),'Log Off')]> is not present
(14ms)
  X NightwatchAssertError
   Testing if element <//*[contains(text(),'Log Off')]> is present in
5000ms - expected "is present" but got: "not present" (5183ms)
    Error location:
    D:\WORK\BPB PUBLICATIONS\NIGHTWATCH\BPBNightWatchProject\nightwatch\
examples\codeexamplesbook\chapter13-loginDataTest.js:30
    ─────────────────────────────────────────────────────────────────
─────────────────────────────────────────────────────
    28 |            .setValue("//input[@name='password']", row.password)
    29 |            .click("//button[@id='tdb5']")
    30 |            .assert.elementPresent("//*[contains(text(),'Log Off')]")
```

```
  31 |              .click('link text', 'Log Off')
  32 |              .click('link text', 'Continue')

  ---------------------------------------------------------------------
---------------------------------------------------------

FAILED: 1 assertions failed and  2 passed (13.887s)
```

```
TEST FAILURE (15.262s):
  - 1 assertions failed; 2 passed
  × 1) codeexamplesbook\chapter13-loginDataTest
  - Login Logout with Data (13.887s)
  → X NightwatchAssertError
  Testing if element <//*[contains(text(),'Log Off')]> is present in
5000ms - expected "is present" but got: "not present" (5183ms)
  Error location:
  D:\WORK\BPB PUBLICATIONS\NIGHTWATCH\BPBNightWatchProject\nightwatch\
examples\codeexamplesbook\chapter13-loginDataTest.js:30

  ---------------------------------------------------------------------
---------------------------------------------------------

  28 |              .setValue("//input[@name='password']", row.password)
  29 |              .click("//button[@id='tdb5']")
  30 |              .assert.elementPresent("//*[contains(text(),'Log Off')]")
  31 |              .click('link text', 'Log Off')
  32 |              .click('link text', 'Continue')

  ---------------------------------------------------------------------
---------------------------------------------------------

Wrote HTML report file to: D:\WORK\BPB PUBLICATIONS\NIGHTWATCH\
BPBNightWatchProject\tests_output\nightwatch-html-report\index.html
```

Note: Depending on the location of the project in your system, the path information mentioned here will change.

Thus, with this, we have seen how to write and read data from a CSV file. We have also seen how to read the data from the CSV file and pass that information to the login logout test script, which then performs the execution on the application. In the next section, we will see how to read and write data in an Excel file and use it in our tests.

Read and write Excel files

An Excel file is a spreadsheet file (commonly with extensions like **.xlsx** or **.xls**) that stores data in a structured grid of rows and columns within worksheets. Each worksheet can contain data, formulas, formatting, and other features. Unlike plain text files, Excel files allow you to customize cell formatting, perform calculations with functions, create charts, and organize data across multiple sheets.

Excel files are widely used for storing, analyzing, and visualizing data. Due of their versatility, they are often employed in test automation projects to keep test data, expected results, or configuration details. This allows scripts to read and update information in a dynamic way. In this section, we will see how to write data in an Excel file and read information from it. Once we understand these operations, we will explore how to incorporate Excel file handling into our test automation framework.

The following is an illustration of what a sample Excel file might look like in Microsoft Excel:

	A	B
1	email	password
2	bpb@bpb.com	bpb@123
3	error@error.com	error@123
4		

***Figure 13.5**: Excel file with data of email and password*

In the preceding figure, the first column represents the options of data to be entered, i.e., email, and password. From the second row, we have the actual data values present in the sheet. So, like the section above, where we handle reading data from the CSV file, we will do the same for the Excel file here. Just read the data into the array and pass it to the login logout script which performs the action on the application.

Writing Excel files

To write an Excel file, we first need to initialize a new workbook (or open an existing one). Once the workbook is created, we can add one or more worksheets with the desired data. The write method will create (or overwrite) the target file if it exists. Some libraries also allow appending or modifying existing workbooks, but for simplicity, we will overwrite if the file already exists. To work with Excel file, we will use the **`xlsx`** module of the Node.js. For this, we need to install it using the command: **`npm install xlsx`**

The following is a sample code snippet that creates an Excel file called **`data.xlsx`** containing user login details to be used for the BPB practice application:

```
const XLSX = require("xlsx");
// Define the data we want to write to the Excel file.
// This format is known as "AOA" (array of arrays):
const data = [
  ["email", "password"],
  ["bpb@bpb.com", "bpb@123"],
```

```
    ["error@error.com", "error@123"]
];
// 1. Create a new workbook
const workbook = XLSX.utils.book_new();
// 2. Convert our data into a worksheet
const worksheet = XLSX.utils.aoa_to_sheet(data);
// 3. Append the worksheet to the workbook
XLSX.utils.book_append_sheet(workbook, worksheet, "Users");
// 4. Write the workbook to an Excel file
XLSX.writeFile(workbook, "data.xlsx");
console.log("Excel file created: data.xlsx");
```

This will generate a file named **data.xlsx** in your project folder. If you open **data.xlsx** in Excel (or another compatible spreadsheet program), you will see the following rows and columns populated:

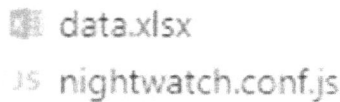

Figure 13.6: data.xlsx file created on code execution

We will now see how to read data from this Excel file in the following section.

Reading Excel files

Once we have our Excel data file generated (e.g., **data.xlsx**), we can use the following code to read and display its contents.

```
const XLSX = require("xlsx");
// Load the Excel file
const workbook = XLSX.readFile("data.xlsx");
// Get the first worksheet
const firstSheetName = workbook.SheetNames[0];
const worksheet = workbook.Sheets[firstSheetName];
// Convert the worksheet to a 2D array (array of arrays)
const data = XLSX.utils.sheet_to_json(worksheet, { header: 1 });
// Option 1: Stringify the data to see all values
console.log(JSON.stringify(data, null, 2));
// Option 2: Log each row in a more readable way
data.forEach((row, rowIndex) => {
  console.log(`Row ${rowIndex}:`, row);
});
```

When you run this code, you should see the contents of **data.xlsx** printed in your console, similar to this (depending on your data and the sheet's content):

```
PS D:\WORK\BPB PUBLICATIONS\NIGHTWATCH\BPBNightWatchProject> npx nightwatch .\nightwatch\examples\codeexamplesbook\readExcelFile.js
[
  [
    "email",
    "password"
  ],
  [
    "bpb@bpb.com",
    "bpb@123"
  ],
  [
    "error@error.com",
    "error@123"
  ]
]
Row 0: [ 'email', 'password' ]
Row 1: [ 'bpb@bpb.com', 'bpb@123' ]
Row 2: [ 'error@error.com', 'error@123' ]
```

Figure 13.7: Data from the Excel file

Thus, with the help of the preceding code, we can read the data from the Excel file and print it in the console.

Creating login logout with Excel data

Based on the information above, we will create scripts to read data from the Excel file. For that, we will create a **dataReaderExcel.js** file, which will, in a similar manner to a CSV file, read the data and create a function that returns an array where data is stored. We will then create another script that will perform the actual login logout function on the application. The code to read data from an Excel file and store in array which will be returned by the function, is as follows:

```
const XLSX = require('xlsx');
function readDataFromExcel(filePath, sheetName) {
  return new Promise((resolve, reject) => {
    try {
      const workbook = XLSX.readFile(filePath);
      const worksheet = workbook.Sheets[sheetName];
      if (!worksheet) {
        return reject(new Error(`Worksheet "${sheetName}" not found in
${filePath}`));
      }
      // Convert worksheet to an array of arrays (row-by-row)
      const aoaData = XLSX.utils.sheet_to_json(worksheet, { header: 1 });
      // If only headers or empty
```

```
      if (aoaData.length < 2) {
        return resolve([]);
      }
      const headers = aoaData[0];        // The header row
      const rows = aoaData.slice(1);     // Remaining rows are data
      // Convert each row array into an object using the headers
      const dataObjects = rows.map((row) => {
        const rowObject = {};
        headers.forEach((header, index) => {
          // Ensure property name matches exactly what's in the header row
          rowObject[header] = row[index] ? row[index].toString().trim() :
"";
        });
        return rowObject;
      });
      resolve(dataObjects);
    } catch (error) {
      reject(error);
    }
  });
}
module.exports = { readDataFromExcel };
```

Once we have read the data, and created the function **readDataFromExcel**, we can now create the login logout script, which will call this function. The test will iterate for as many rows as available with the Excel file. The script is as follows:

```
const { readDataFromExcel } = require('./dataReaderExcel.js');
describe('Login Logout BPB', function() {
  let credentials = [];
  // Load Excel data before starting the test
  before(function(browser, done) {
    readDataFromExcel('D:\\WORK\\BPB PUBLICATIONS\\NIGHTWATCH\\
BPBNightWatchProject\\data.xlsx','Users')
      .then(data => {
        credentials = data;
        done();  // Tell Nightwatch we're done with async setup
      })
      .catch(err => {
        done(err); // Pass any error to Nightwatch
```

```
        });
    });

    it('Login Logout with Data', function(browser) {
        // For each row in the spreadsheet, do a login-logout cycle
        credentials.forEach((row, index) => {
            browser
                .useXpath()
                .navigateTo('http://practice.bpbonline.com/')
                .click('link text', 'My Account')
                .setValue("//input[@name='email_address']", row.email)
                .setValue("//input[@name='password']", row.password)
                .click("//button[@id='tdb5']")
                .assert.elementPresent("//*[contains(text(),'Log Off')]")
                .click('link text', 'Log Off')
                .click('link text', 'Continue')
                .assert.not.elementPresent("//*[contains(text(),'Log Off')]");
        });
    });
    // Close the browser after the tests finish
    after(browser => browser.end());
});
```

As we execute the preceding script, we will see that our tests execute twice, one for valid user credential, and then for invalid user credential. The output is as follows:

```
PS D:\WORK\BPB PUBLICATIONS\NIGHTWATCH\BPBNightWatchProject> npx nightwatch
.\nightwatch\examples\codeexamplesbook\chapter13-loginExcelDataTest.js
[Login Logout BPB] Test Suite

────────────────────────────────────────────────────────────

⸫ Starting ChromeDriver on port 9515...
i Connected to ChromeDriver on port 9515 (623ms).
  Using: chrome (131.0.6778.266) on WINDOWS.
  Running Login Logout with Data:

────────────────────────────────────────────────────────────


────────────────────────────────
  √ Testing if element <//*[contains(text(),'Log Off')]> is present (29ms)
  √ Testing if element <//*[contains(text(),'Log Off')]> is not present
(32ms)
  X NightwatchAssertError
```

Testing if element <//*[contains(text(),'Log Off')]> is present in
5000ms - expected "is present" but got: "not present" (5227ms)
    Error location:
    D:\WORK\BPB PUBLICATIONS\NIGHTWATCH\BPBNightWatchProject\nightwatch\
examples\codeexamplesbook\chapter13-loginExcelDataTest.js:28

----
    26 | .setValue("//input[@name='password']", row.password)
    27 | .click("//button[@id='tdb5']")
    28 | .assert.elementPresent("//*[contains(text(),'Log Off')]")
    29 | .click('link text', 'Log Off')
    30 | .click('link text', 'Continue')

  FAILED: 1 assertions failed and 2 passed (13.975s)

  TEST FAILURE (15.517s):
   - 1 assertions failed; 2 passed
   × 1) codeexamplesbook\chapter13-loginExcelDataTest
   - Login Logout with Data (13.975s)
   → X NightwatchAssertError
   Testing if element <//*[contains(text(),'Log Off')]> is present in
5000ms - expected "is present" but got: "not present" (5227ms)
    Error location:
    D:\WORK\BPB PUBLICATIONS\NIGHTWATCH\BPBNightWatchProject\nightwatch\
examples\codeexamplesbook\chapter13-loginExcelDataTest.js:28

----
    26 | .setValue("//input[@name='password']", row.password)
    27 | .click("//button[@id='tdb5']")
    28 | .assert.elementPresent("//*[contains(text(),'Log Off')]")
    29 | .click('link text', 'Log Off')
    30 | .click('link text', 'Continue')

 Wrote HTML report file to: D:\WORK\BPB PUBLICATIONS\NIGHTWATCH\
BPBNightWatchProject\tests_output\nightwatch-html-report\index.html

Thus, with the preceding code, we can parameterize the login logout test by reading data from csv and Excel file, respectively, and iterate the test for as many data rows as available with the file.

Conclusion

In this chapter, we explored how to use data files—first in CSV format and then in Excel—to drive test automation scripts. We covered creating the data file, writing code to read and parse that file, and integrating the data within a simple Nightwatch test to execute login/logout steps. By separating data handling from the test scripts themselves, we achieve a more maintainable and flexible approach that can easily adapt to multiple test scenarios or varied data sets.

You learned how libraries such as xlsx can simplify reading from Excel files, how to troubleshoot common pitfalls (such as incorrect sheet names or mismatched headers), and how to ensure the data you read is passed correctly to your test logic. With these techniques, your automation tests can more efficiently handle varied inputs, making them robust and scalable. As a next step, you can incorporate advanced framework design patterns (such as Page Objects) or enhance error handling to evolve your test suite into a full-fledged, professional-grade automation framework.

In the next chapter, we will learn about logs and capturing screenshots.

Questions

1. What advantages does storing test data in an Excel file offer over a simple CSV file, and what library do we commonly use in Node.js to handle Excel files?

2. In the provided examples, how do we convert the Excel spreadsheet data into an array of objects (where each object represents a row) so that Nightwatch can iterate through and use the data for login tests?

3. Why is it important to check that the Excel sheet's first row exactly matches the property names (e.g., email and password) in the code, and what happens if these header names do not match?

Answers

1. Storing test data has the following advantages:

   a. Excel files allow for more complex data organization (multiple sheets, built-in formatting, formulas, etc.).

   b. They can store different data sets in different worksheets within the same file, making them easier to manage for larger or more structured test data.

2. In Node.js, the popular library to handle Excel files is **xlsx**. It provides functions to read from and write to Excel files in various formats (e.g., .xlsx, .xls).

   By using XLSX.utils.sheet_to_json, which reads the worksheet and automatically interprets the first row as the header row. Each subsequent row is mapped to an object whose keys are taken from the header cells (e.g., email, password) and whose values are the data in the corresponding cells.

   For instance, if the first row is ["email", "password"] and the next rows contain user credentials, and the result will be an array like:

```js
Copy
[
  { email: "bpb@bpb.com", password: "bpb@123" },
  { email: "error@error.com", password: "error@123" }
]
```

   This makes it straightforward to iterate through each user's credentials in a Nightwatch test.

3. **Importance**: The code that reads the Excel data relies on the first row to map column values to object properties. If the header row does not match the expected property names (e.g., it uses Email address instead of email), the resulting objects might have different keys—or be empty—leading to undefined values in the test.

   Consequence: If the header names do not match, the test will not find row.email or row.password, causing login attempts to fail or skip the data entirely. Essentially, any mismatch in headers can break the link between the spreadsheet columns and the code's expected object properties.

Join our book's Discord space

Join the book's Discord Workspace for Latest updates, Offers, Tech happenings around the world, New Release and Sessions with the Authors:

https://discord.bpbonline.com

CHAPTER 14

Learn About Logs, and Screenshots Management

In the previous few chapters, we discussed various components that should be implemented at the test automation architecture level to make the test automation scripts and suite more robust and scalable for the future. We discussed object management through the page object model, data management using external data files like CSV, Excel, and how we can use the data from these files and pass it to the scripts. In this chapter, we will discuss another important component, which is logs, capturing screenshots for better reporting of bugs, and the status of product health under test.

Test automation involves running a suite of tests to validate the functionality and stability of software applications. However, as test suites grow more complex, it becomes increasingly important to record what happens during each test execution. Logs and screenshots are two essential artifacts that can help you diagnose issues quickly and record how tests behave over time. This chapter covers best practices, common tools, and how to incorporate logging and screenshot management into your automation framework.

Structure

This chapter will have the following sections:

- Capturing logs and screenshots
- Understand logs
- Generating and managing logs
- Screenshot management

Objectives

By the end of this chapter, you will be able to understand how to capture logs and screenshots during test execution. We will explore how to interpret logs, generate and manage them efficiently, and also cover methods for managing screenshots.

Capturing logs and screenshots

In any test automation strategy, it is not enough to know whether a test passed or failed. You need details: why a test failed, where it failed, what the application looked like at the time of failure, and how to reproduce or debug the problem. Logs and screenshots are the primary means to capture that information. Logs capture real-time messages about the test steps, environment states, console outputs, and error stacks. Screenshots provide visual confirmation of the application state at a point in time, especially useful for GUI-based tests. When integrated properly, these artifacts can drastically reduce the time it takes to diagnose test failures and maintain the automation suite.

Understanding logs

Logs are records of events, statuses, or errors that occur during the execution of a program. In test automation, logs can include:

- Test steps: For example, Clicked on Login button.
- Assertions: For example, Verified Log Off element is present.
- Debug messages: For example, Parsed user data: {email: ..., password: ...}.
- System or browser messages: For example, network requests, console errors.

Now, let us see why logs are important:

- **Debugging**: If a test fails, logs can pinpoint the step at which things went wrong.
- **Traceability**: Logs show the chronological order of events, helping you understand the flow of test execution.
- **Compliance and reporting**: Some organizations require a record of all test runs for audit or compliance purposes.
- **Continuous improvement**: By reviewing logs regularly, you can identify patterns (e.g., flaky tests) and improve test stability.

We can capture various types of logs. The following list explains these types:

- **Console logs**: Messages printed by the application or the test framework.
- **Browser logs (for web apps)**: Captured from the browser's console (e.g., JavaScript errors).

- **Server logs**: Captured from the back-end if you have access (e.g., network errors, exceptions).
- **Custom logs**: Messages you explicitly add within your test code or page objects (e.g., using **console.log** in Node.js or specialized logging frameworks like Winston/Pino).

Generating and managing logs

In the above actions, we understood the need for logs. We also understood where logs help us get access to more information, which helps us debug the underlying problem. We have also seen the types of logs that can be made available. We have concise logs or more detailed ones, depending on the stage of development we are in. These log level settings are generally maintained as configuration settings.

In this section, let us see how to generate the logs and their types:

Basic logging with console.log

The simplest approach is to use **console.log** (and variants like **console.warn**, **console. error**) within your test scripts:

```
it("Console Logs Example", function(browser) {
    console.log("Starting the sample test...");

    browser
      .navigateTo("https://nightwatchjs.org/")
      .perform(() => console.log("Navigated to example.com"))
      .assert.titleContains("Nightwatch");

    console.log("Sample test completed.");
  });
```

This outputs the logs to the console, as follows:

```
[Codeexamplesbook\chapter14 Console Logs] Test Suite
```

```
⋮ Starting ChromeDriver on port 9515...
DevTools listening on ws://127.0.0.1:63178/devtools/browser/b6759694-a2b8-
455b-923f-f99aef1b1988
DevTools listening on ws://127.0.0.1:63178/devtools/browser/b6759694-a2b8-
455b-923f-f99aef1b1988
DevTools listening on ws://127.0.0.1:63178/devtools/browser/b6759694-a2b8-
```

```
455b-923f-f99aef1b1988
DevTools listening on ws://127.0.0.1:63178/devtools/browser/b6750694-a2b8-
455b-923f-f99aef1b1988
DevTools listening on ws://127.0.0.1:63178/devtools/browser/b6750694-a2b8-
455b-923f-f99aef1b1988
i Connected to ChromeDriver on port 9515 (1010ms).
  Using: chrome (131.0.6778.266) on WINDOWS.
  Running Console Logs Example:
```

```
Starting the sample test...
Sample test completed.
Navigated to example.com
  √ Testing if the page title contains 'Nightwatch' (19ms)
  ⊠ PASSED. 1 assertions. (1.963s)
 Wrote HTML report file to: D:\WORK\BPB PUBLICATIONS\NIGHTWATCH\
BPBNightWatchProject\tests_output\nightwatch-html-report\index.html
```

We can find in the output the console log message we have printed. Next, we will use a log library to generate and manage logs.

Using a logging library

For advanced logs generation and management, we will use Winston, a popular logger library for Node.js. You can find more information about it here: **https://github.com/winstonjs/winston**.

Now, let us see how to set it up:

1. The first step will be to install the **winston** module. For this, we will use the following command:

   workingdir:/> npm install Winston

2. After installing **winston**, we will now use the module in the code to generate logs both for the console and the file. The script for it is as follows:

```javascript
const winston = require("winston");
const logger = winston.createLogger({
  level: 'info',
  transports: [
    new winston.transports.Console(),
    new winston.transports.File({ filename: 'automation.log' })
  ]
```

```
});
logger.info("Starting test suite...");
logger.error("An error occurred while logging in!");
```

3. As we execute the preceding code, we will see that the log message is generated in the console, and also an **automation.log** gets created in the file system. The following screenshot displays it. Let us first see the console message:

PS D:\WORK\BPB PUBLICATIONS\NIGHTWATCH\BPBNightWatchProject> npx nightwatch .\nightwatch\examples\codeexamplesbook\chapter14-generateLogsWinston.js

Debugger attached.

Debugger attached.

{"level":"info","message":"Starting test suite..."**}**

{"level":"error","message":"An error occurred while logging in!"**}**

4. Simultaneously, a new file will be created in the directory. The file name will be **automation.log**. Let us see the contents of the file:

```
automation.log
1    {"level":"info","message":"Starting test suite..."}
2    {"level":"error","message":"An error occurred while logging in!"}
```

Figure 14.1: Automation log file

5. As we can see in the preceding figure, there is information on the level of log being generated, which is, info and error. It is followed by the message we want to generate for the log detail. With the help of this basic example, we can understand how to use the **winston** module for log.

6. Now, let us see the login logout script. With the logs, we will also have the script pick data from an external data source which is a **.csv** file and will have page object used as well.

```
/*
   Login Logout with Page Object Model, Data From CSV and Logging
*/
const winston = require("winston");
const logger = winston.createLogger({
  level: 'info',
  transports: [
    new winston.transports.Console(),
    new winston.transports.File({ filename: 'loginlogouttest.log' })
  ]
```

```
});
const { readDataFromCSV } = require('./dataReader.js');
describe('Login Logout BPB', function() {
  let credentials = [];
  // Load CSV data before starting the test
  before(function(browser, done) {
    readDataFromCSV('D:\\WORK\\BPB PUBLICATIONS\\NIGHTWATCH\\
BPBNightWatchProject\\nightwatch\\examples\\codeexamplesbook\\data.
csv')  // <-- Make sure your CSV file name/path is correct
      .then(data => {
        credentials = data;
        done();  // Tell Nightwatch we're done with async setup
      })
      .catch(err => {
        done(err); // Pass any error to Nightwatch
      });
  });
  it('Login Logout with Data', function(browser) {
    logger.info("Starting Loging Logout.. ");
    credentials.forEach((row, index) => {
      browser
        .useXpath()
        const homepage = browser.page.bpbpractice.homepage(); //
home page object
        homepage.navigate();
        homepage.click('@myAccountLink');
        const loginpage = browser.page.bpbpractice.loginpage(); //
login page object
        loginpage.assert.elementPresent("@username_txtbox"); //
asserting element presence
        logger.info("verifying we are on login page..");
        loginpage.login(row.email,row.password);
        //logout page object
        const logoutpage = browser.page.bpbpractice.logoutpage(); //
logout page object
        logoutpage.logout();
        logger.info("Test complete for user details, username: " +
row.email + " and password: " + row.password);
```

```
      });
    });
    // After hook to capture errors and close the browser
    after(function(browser, done) {
      // Access the test results
      const results = browser.currentTest.results;
      // Check for failed assertions or errors
      if (results.failed > 0 || results.errors > 0) {
        logger.error('Test had a failing assertion or an error.');
      }
      // Close the browser
      browser.end(() => {
        if (typeof done === 'function') {
          done();
        }
      });
    });
  });
});
```

The page objects code above are the same scripts we generated in *Chapter 12, Page Objects*. The data reading files are the same as those we generated in *Chapter 13, Managing Data Using Excel and CSV Files*.

As we execute the code, we will find the data being read from the **.csv** file, **data.csv** with the following contents:

```
nightwatch > examples > codeexamplesbook > 🖩 data.csv > 🗋 data
1     email,password
2     bpb@bpb.com,bpb@123
3     someone@example.com,junk
```

Figure 14.2: data.csv file

The first line of the file contains the names of the data pointers, where the first column is email and the second is password. The file has a row of valid user credentials and another row of invalid user credentials. When we execute the script, we get the **loginlogouttest.log** file generated.

The contents of the file are as follows:

```
loginlogouttest.log
1    {"level":"info","message":"Starting Loging Logout.. "}
2    {"level":"info","message":"verifying we are on login page.."}
3    {"level":"info","message":"Test complete for user details, username: bpb@bpb.com and password: bpb@123"}
4    {"level":"info","message":"verifying we are on login page.."}
5    {"level":"info","message":"Test complete for user details, username: someone@example.com and password: junk"}
6    {"level":"error","message":"Test had a failing assertion or an error."}
```

Figure 14.3: loginlogout.log file contents

As seen in the log contents, we will find that it is reporting the assertion error. It is good to note here that we can further improve these files, add exception handling, and logs at lower-level files as well, to capture more details. That is an exercise best left to the reader.

In the previous sections, we learned about logging, the need for it, and how to implement it. We have also seen various log levels that we can come across and use them in our scripts accordingly. Let us now have a look at some of the best practices we can follow:

- **Use meaningful messages**: Instead of `console.log("Test started")`, prefer something descriptive like `logger.info("Starting login test with user: " + username)`.

- **Avoid over-logging**: Too many logs can obscure important details. Log at key steps or error points.

- **Log levels**: Adopt a consistent logging level strategy. For instance, debug for in-depth dev logs, info for high-level steps, and error for failures or exceptions.

- **Prefix logs**: If you run multiple tests in parallel, prefix logs with the test name or ID to separate them easily.

Screenshot management

When creating test automation suites, and executing them, most of the time, the executions happen unattended. In this situation, if the test fails, we would want to know the reason for the failure and capture a screenshot, which provides more details about why the failure occurred, and what the state of the application was when the test failed. All the information, including logs and screenshots, will help with debugging the errors that are generated while the application is under test.

The need for screenshots

A screenshot provides a snapshot of the application's UI at a specific moment, which is valuable for:

- **Visual confirmation**: Verifying if the UI is in the correct state (e.g., an error message is present).

- **Debugging UI issues**: Locating an unexpected pop-up, misaligned element, or styling issue.

- **Documentation**: Attaching screenshots to bug tickets or reports to illustrate the problem clearly.

When to capture screenshots

Let us understand where to capture the screenshots:

- **On failure**: Automatically take a screenshot whenever a test or assertion fails. This is the most common approach.

- **After each step**: Capture at every step for highly detailed debugging (though this can be storage-intensive).

- **On demand**: Manually trigger screenshots in your code wherever you suspect issues.

In the previous sections, we understood why screenshot capturing is required and the value it brings. Now, let us understand how we can capture screenshots and enrich our tests using Nightwatch.

Capturing screenshots in Nightwatch

Nightwatch provides a built-in command called **browser.saveScreenshot()**. We can use this method to capture a screenshot of the page where the execution is taking place. It will capture the screenshot and save it in the folder location we provide. To know more about this method, you can see this link: **https://nightwatchjs.org/api/saveScreenshot.html**

With the help of the following code, we can take the preceding example of the login logout script we made enriched with page objects and data handling now. In the same script, we will add the following lines to capture the screenshot, after my account link is clicked, and login logout action is done:

```
//my account
homepage.click('@myAccountLink');
browser.saveScreenshot("screenshots/myaccountpage.png")
//login
loginpage.login(row.email,row.password);
const screenshotname="screenshots/loginpage" +row.email + ".png"
browser.saveScreenshot(screenshotname)
//logout
logoutpage.logout();
browser.saveScreenshot("screenshots/logout.png")
```

When these commands are executed, they will generate and save the screenshots in the screenshot folder, which will be created inside the project. The contents will look as the following figure. The images might not be clearly visible, but the point is to mention that multiple images exist:

Figure 14.4: Captured screenshots

Conclusion

Logs and screenshots are the backbone of effective debugging in test automation. Combining descriptive log messages with timely screenshots gives you a clear view of what occurred before and during test failures. This visibility drastically reduces the time to find and fix issues, making your suite more robust and less prone to mystery errors.

With a strong logging and screenshot management strategy in place, your test automation framework becomes more transparent and easier to maintain, allowing your team to focus on writing new tests and improving product quality, rather than tracking down elusive bugs.

In the next chapter, we will see how to set up Nightwatch using browser stack automation on cloud infrastructure for test executions.

Questions

1. Why are logs and screenshots both critical for diagnosing issues in automated tests?

2. How can you run scalable tests?

Answers

1. Logs and screenshots are critical to diagnose issues in automated tests, as most tests are executed in unattended mode. And when failure happens, the information captured in logs and automated tests helps us to debug.

2. To run scalable tests, we can use a cloud service provider, for example, with Nightwatch, we can use BrowserStack or Sauce Labs to do executions.

CHAPTER 15

Execution of Tests in BrowserStack

In the world of web development, ensuring that the application performs consistently across various browsers and devices is crucial. This is where testing products well comes into the picture. Automation to achieve quality testing and faster effort is required, and that is where tools like Nightwatch have a role to play. Nightwatch, as we have seen in this book, is a Selenium-based test automation framework, based on the WebDriver protocol. Selenium is a browser automation library, and tools like Nightwatch provide various capabilities and features that enable end users to use the power of Selenium for test automation purposes.

One of the activities in test automation that we have to perform is the execution of the tests. Execution of the test is a demanding process. We would like to test our application on all platforms where our end users are using it. However, in today's frequent releases and bug fixes, it is demanding to maintain our own test automation labs. That is where cloud service providers like Sauce Labs, BrowserStack, and similar organizations come into the picture. You can definitely have your own, but knowing that a solution exists always helps.

In this chapter, we will explore BrowserStack as a solution for our test execution needs since Browser Stack supports the Nightwatch project and builds it for Open Source.

Note: Other similar organizations also support test executions built-in Nightwatch on their platforms because they support Selenium.

BrowserStack, a cloud-based cross-browser testing platform, empowers developers and testers to execute tests on a wide array of real browsers, operating systems, and mobile devices without the need for maintaining an extensive local testing infrastructure.

Integrating Nightwatch.js with BrowserStack combines the robust end-to-end testing capabilities of Nightwatch with the comprehensive cross-browser support of BrowserStack. This chapter will guide you through setting up and executing your Nightwatch tests on BrowserStack, enabling you to achieve higher test coverage and enhanced reliability. To know more about BrowserStack, visit this link: **https://www.browserstack.com/**.

Structure

In this chapter, we will discuss the following topics:

- Prerequisites for setting test execution on BrowserStack
- Setting up a BrowserStack account
- Installing required dependencies
- Configuring Nightwatch for BrowserStack
- Executing tests on BrowserStack
- Viewing and analyzing test results

Objectives

By the end of this chapter, you will be able to understand the prerequisites for setting up test execution on BrowserStack. We will explore setting up a BrowserStack account, installing the required dependencies, and configuring Nightwatch for BrowserStack. You will also learn about executing tests on BrowserStack and viewing and analyzing the test results.

Prerequisites for setting test execution on BrowserStack

Before diving into executing Nightwatch tests on BrowserStack, ensure that you have the following:

- **Node.js and npm installed**: Nightwatch.js is a Node.js-based testing framework. Ensure you have Node.js (version 14.x or later) and **npm** installed on your machine.
- **Nightwatch.js installed**: If you have not installed Nightwatch.js yet, you can do so using **npm:**
  bash
  Copy
  ```
  npm install nightwatch --save-dev
  ```

- **BrowserStack account**: A BrowserStack account is required to access their cloud-based testing infrastructure. To begin with start with creation of a free account.

- **Basic knowledge of Nightwatch.js**: Familiarity with writing and running Nightwatch tests will be beneficial. By now, you should be equipped with this knowledge.

Setting up a BrowserStack account

To begin, you need to set up a BrowserStack account and obtain your **Access Key** and **Username**, which are essential for authentication. Follow these steps to set up a BrowserStack account:

1. **Sign up or Log in**: Visit BrowserStack and sign up for an account or log in if you already have one.

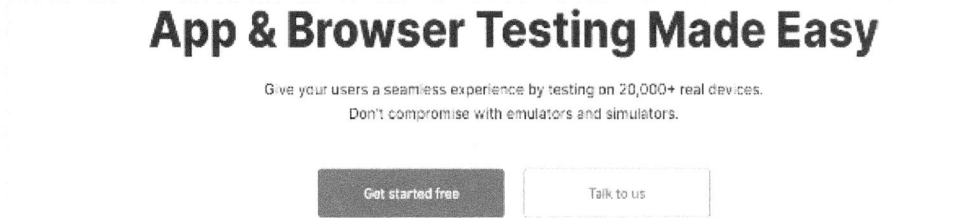

Figure 15.1: *BrowserStack account creation page*

2. Click on the **Get Started** free button, and fill in the details of the web page, as shown in the following figure:

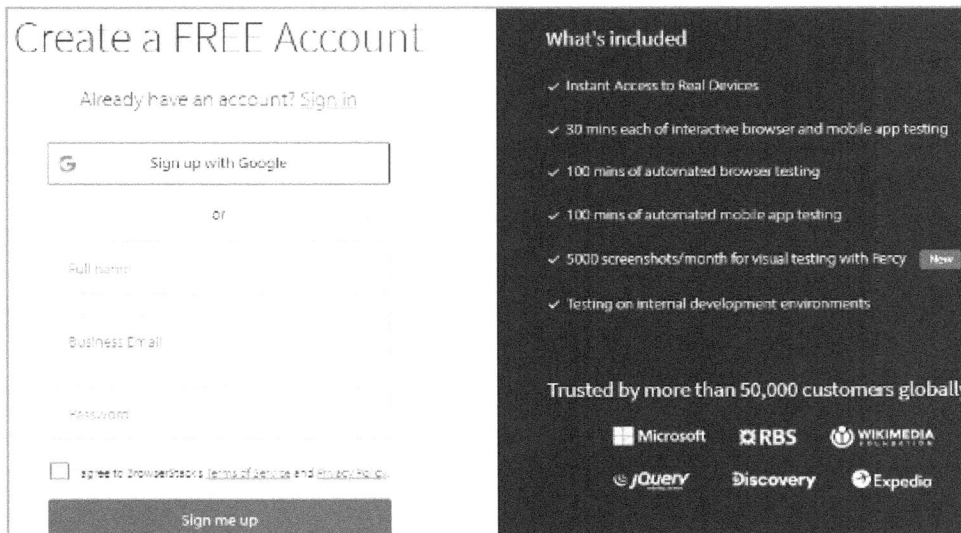

Figure 15.2: *Free Account creation page*

3. Navigate to account settings:

   a. Click on your profile avatar in the top-right corner.

   b. Select **Account Settings** from the dropdown.

4. Retrieve credentials:

   a. Under the **Access Keys** section, you will find your **Username** and **Access Key**.

      Note: Keep these credentials secure. They are required for authenticating API requests.

The following figure shows the details about Account credentials. Please note that the actual username and key are hidden in the image. You should be able to create the BrowserStack account and then go to your Account Profile to access that information.

Figure 15.3: Credential information

Installing required dependencies

To integrate Nightwatch with BrowserStack, you need to install additional dependencies and ensure that your project is correctly configured.

1. Install Nightwatch and related packages:

   a. If you have not installed Nightwatch yet, do so now:

   ```bash
   Copy
   npm install nightwatch --save-dev
   ```

   b. Additionally, install the Selenium WebDriver (https://www.selenium.dev/) if necessary, although BrowserStack manages the Selenium server for you.

2. Install **browserstack-local** (Optional):

   If your tests require access to local or staging environments not publicly accessible, install the browserstack-local package:

   ```bash
   Copy
   npm install browserstack-local --save-dev
   ```

This allows BrowserStack to establish a secure connection to your local machine.

Configuring Nightwatch for BrowserStack

Configuring Nightwatch to work with BrowserStack involves setting up your **nightwatch. conf.js** (or **nightwatch.json**) configuration file with the necessary BrowserStack credentials and desired capabilities.

1. Obtain BrowserStack credentials:

   From your BrowserStack account settings, copy your username and access key. These will be used for authentication.

2. Update Nightwatch configuration:

   Create or update your **nightwatch.conf.js** file with BrowserStack settings. The following is a sample configuration:

```
const additonalEnvironments = require("./environments");
if(!additonalEnvironments.test_settings)
  additonalEnvironments.test_settings = {};
const bstackOptions = {
  'bstack:options' : {
    "os" : "OS X",
    "osVersion" : "OS",
    "buildName" : "NightwatchDemo-1",
    "sessionName" : "gtr-workshop-nightwatch",
    "source": "nightwatch:sample-sdk:v1.0",
    "seleniumVersion" : "4.0.0",
    userName: '${BROWSERSTACK_USERNAME}' || 'USERNAME',
    accessKey: '${BROWSERSTACK_ACCESS_KEY}' || 'ACCESS_KEY',
  },
}
const browserStack = {
  webdriver: {
    start_process: false,
    timeout_options: {
      timeout: 120000,
      retry_attempts: 3
    },
    keep_alive: true
  },
```

```
  selenium: {
    host: 'hub.browserstack.com',
    port: 443
  },
  desiredCapabilities: {
    browserName: 'chrome',
    ...bstackOptions
  }
}
const nightwatchConfigs = {
  src_folders: [],
  live_output: true,
  plugins: ['@nightwatch/browserstack'],
  '@nightwatch/browserstack': {
    browserstackLocal: true // set true to manage browserstack local
tunnel. Defaults to false.
  },
  test_settings: {
    default: {
      launch_url: 'https://nightwatchjs.org'
    },
    browserstack:  {
      ...browserStack
    },
    "browserstack.chrome": {
      ...browserStack,
      desiredCapabilities:{
        browserName: 'chrome',
        ...bstackOptions
      }
    },
    "browserstack.firefox": {
      ...browserStack,
      desiredCapabilities:{
        browserName: 'firefox',
        ...bstackOptions
      }
```

```
        },
        "browserstack.edge": {
          ...browserStack,
          desiredCapabilities:{
            browserName: 'Edge',
            ...bstackOptions
          }
        }
      }
    }
    for(let key in additonalEnvironments.test_settings) {
      nightwatchConfigs.test_settings[key] = {
        ...browserStack,
        ...additonalEnvironments.test_settings[key]
      };
    }
    module.exports = nightwatchConfigs;
```

Before running the execution, in the above configuration file you need to add your username and access key details:

```
userName: '${BROWSERSTACK_USERNAME}' || 'USERNAME',
accessKey: '${BROWSERSTACK_ACCESS_KEY}' || 'ACCESS_KEY',
```

Explanation of configuration fields:

- **selenium_host and selenium_port**: These are set to BrowserStack's Selenium server.

- **username and access_key**: Your BrowserStack credentials. It is recommmended to use environment variables for security.

- **desiredCapabilities**: Defines the browser, version, OS, and other settings for your test sessions.

Executing tests on BrowserStack

With your tests and configuration ready, you can execute them on BrowserStack.

Running a specific test

Use the following command to run a specific test file:

```
npx nightwatch --env browserstack --test tests/loginTest.js
```

We will execute the login logout test, which has been described in *Chapter 8, Assertions* in Nightwatch. The script we will execute is as follows:

```
describe('Login Logout Demosite', function() {
  before(browser => browser.navigateTo('https://5elementslearning.dev/
demosite'));
  it('Login logout Assertion Test', function(browser) {
    browser
    .useXpath() //setting locator to be used as xpath for following
commands
    .click('link text', 'My Account') //click on My Account Link
    .setValue("//input[@name='email_address']", "abc@demo.com")//set email
    .setValue("//input[@name='password']", "demo@123")//set  password
    .click("//button[@id='tdb5']")//click on Sign in button
    //add object presence assertion
    .assert.elementPresent("//*[contains(text(),'Log Off')]")
    .click('link text', 'Log Off')//click on Log Off Link
    .click('link text', 'Continue')// Click on Continue Link
    //add object absence assertion
    .assert.not.elementPresent("//*[contains(text(),'Log Off')]")
  });
  after(browser => browser.end());
});
```

In the preceding script, we are performing login logout on the *BPB* application and using assertion to verify the action being performed. To run the same on different environments, we will use the following command:

npx nightwatch .\test -e env1,env2,env3

When we do this, we can see the execution happening on the BrowserStack account.

Explanation:

- **--env browserstack**: Specifies the testing environment defined in your **nightwatch. conf.js**.

- **--test tests/loginTest.js**: Specifies the test file to execute.

Running all tests

To execute all tests within the **tests/** directory, use this command:

```
npx nightwatch --env browserstack
```

Parallel testing

BrowserStack supports parallel test execution, which can significantly reduce testing time. We can create an environments file called as **environments.js** file. The following shows a sample environment file we can create:

```javascript
module.exports = {
  test_settings: {
    default: {},
    env1: {
      desiredCapabilities: {
        browserName: 'Chrome',
        'bstack:options': {
          browserVersion: '120.0',
          os: 'Windows',
          osVersion: '10',
          debug: true
        }
      }
    },
    env2: {
      desiredCapabilities: {
        browserName: 'Safari',
        'bstack:options': {
          browserVersion: '15.6',
          os: 'OS X',
          osVersion: 'Monterey',
          debug: true
        }
      }
    },
    env3: {
      desiredCapabilities: {
        browserName: 'Chromium',
        'bstack:options': {
          deviceOrientation: 'portrait',
          deviceName: 'iPhone 13',
          osVersion: '15',
          debug: true
        }
      }
```

```
        }
      }
    }
  }
};
```

As we can see in the environment file, there are three environments configured here:

- Windows operating system with Chrome browser

- Mac with Safari

- iPhone 13 with Chromium browser

As the execution starts, we will see the following information on the Command Prompt:

Figure 15.4: Command execution information

Similarly, we can see the execution results on the BrowserStack account as follows:

NightwatchDemo-1

Sessions	6 PASSED	Build Status	⊙ COMPLETED
Last Updated	14 Nov 2024 12:10 UTC	Build ID	9554ffce… ⎙
Duration	55s	Public Link ⊙	Copy Link ⎙

ALL SESSIONS (6)	PASSED (6)	TIMED OUT (0)	ERROR (0)	⇌ Sort	▼ Filter

Session Name	Duration	Status ⊙
gtr-workshop-nightwatch Chrome 120.0 Win 10 · Last updated 6 mins ago	26s	PASSED
gtr-workshop-nightwatch iPhone 13 iOS 15.6 Chromium · Last updated 6 mins ago	25s	PASSED

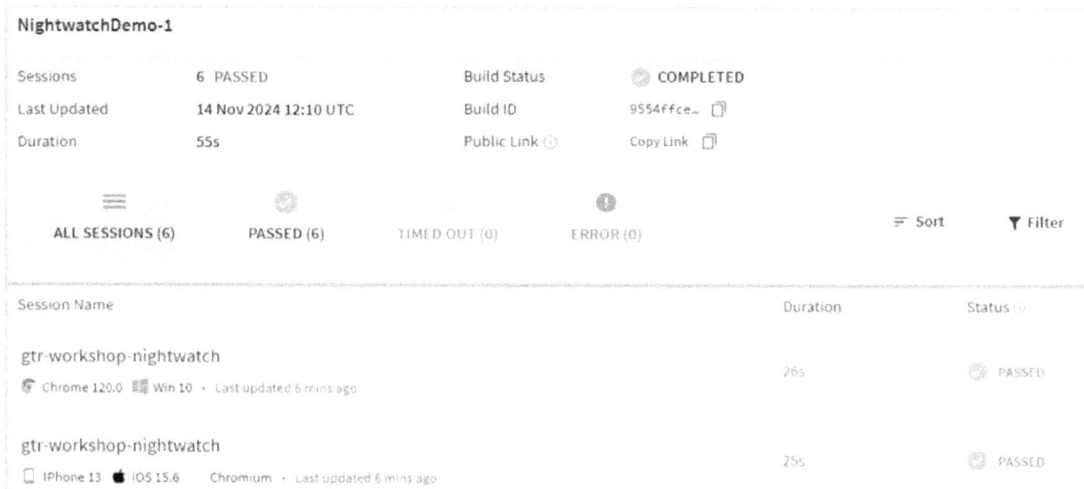

Figure 15.5: Test Execution details from BrowserStack dashboard

The above section explains how we can use BrowserStack to execute tests, define multiple environments, operating systems, and browser configurations, and execute tests on multiple environments.

Viewing and analyzing test results

After executing your tests, BrowserStack provides a comprehensive dashboard to view and analyze the results.

Accessing the dashboard

Follow these steps to access the dashboard:

1. **Log in to BrowserStack**: Navigate to BrowserStack (**https://www.browserstack. com/**) and log in.

2. **Navigate to the Automate dashboard**:

   a. Click on **Automate** in the top navigation bar.

   b. Here, you will see a list of your test sessions.

Viewing test details

Click on a specific test session to view detailed information:

- **Session logs**: Console logs, network logs, and video recordings (if enabled).

- **Screenshots**: Visual snapshots of the application at different stages of the test.

- **Network logs**: Detailed information about network requests made during the test.

Conclusion

Integrating Nightwatch.js with BrowserStack offers a powerful combination for executing robust, cross-browser, and cross-device automated tests. By leveraging BrowserStack's extensive infrastructure and Nightwatch's intuitive testing framework, you can ensure that your web applications deliver a consistent and seamless user experience across diverse environments.

This chapter provided a comprehensive guide to setting up and executing tests on BrowserStack using Nightwatch.js. From configuration to best practices and troubleshooting, you are now equipped to harness the full potential of this integration. As you expand your test suites, remember to adhere to best practices and continuously optimize your tests for efficiency and reliability.

Questions

1. Name other platforms similar to BrowserStack?

2. Can you use a BrowserStack free account to run the same test on multiple environments?

Answers

1. Sauce Labs, LambdaTest, etc.

2. Yes

Join our book's Discord space

Join the book's Discord Workspace for Latest updates, Offers, Tech happenings around the world, New Release and Sessions with the Authors:

https://discord.bpbonline.com

Index

www.ingramcontent.com/pod-product-compliance
Lightning Source LLC
Chambersburg PA
CBHW061813210326
41599CB00034B/6987